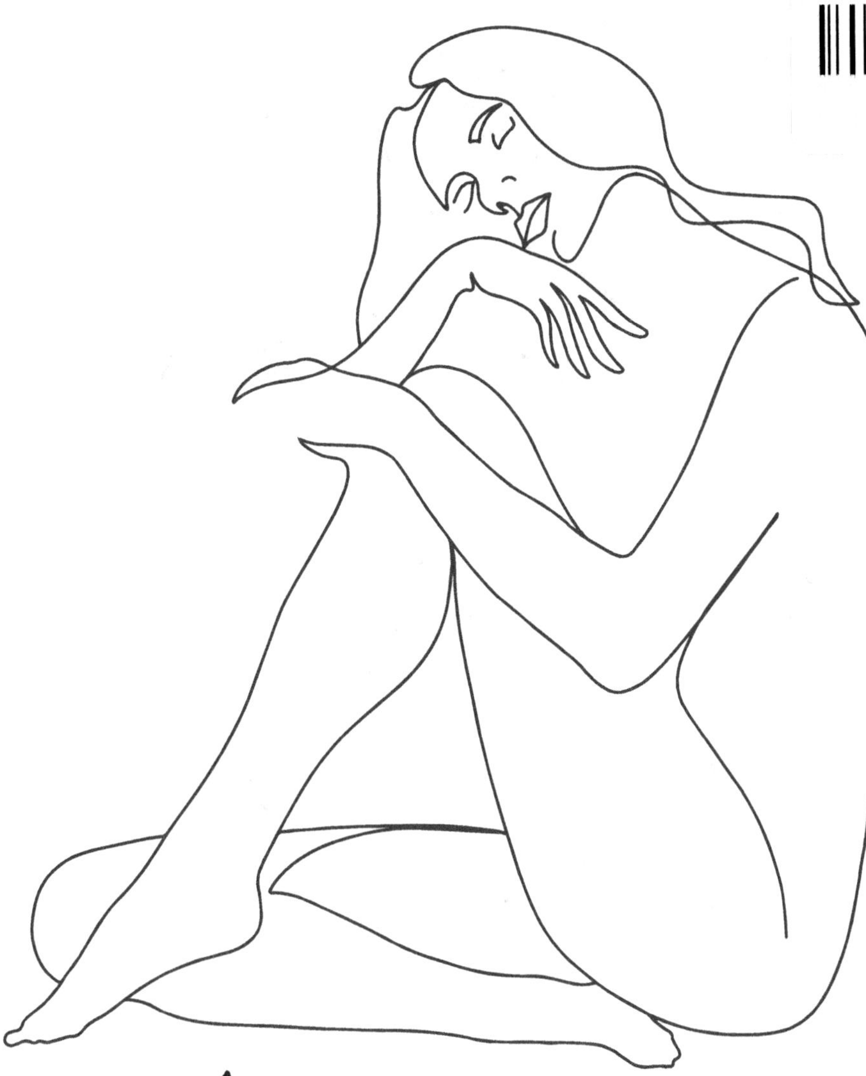

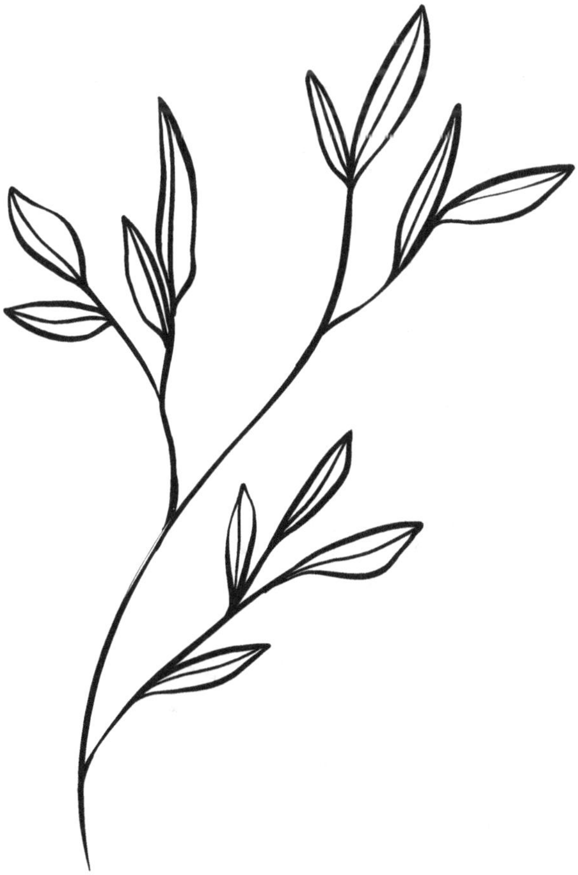

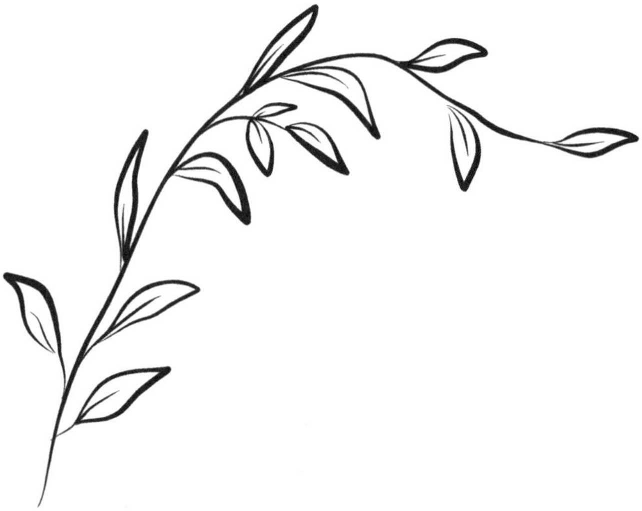

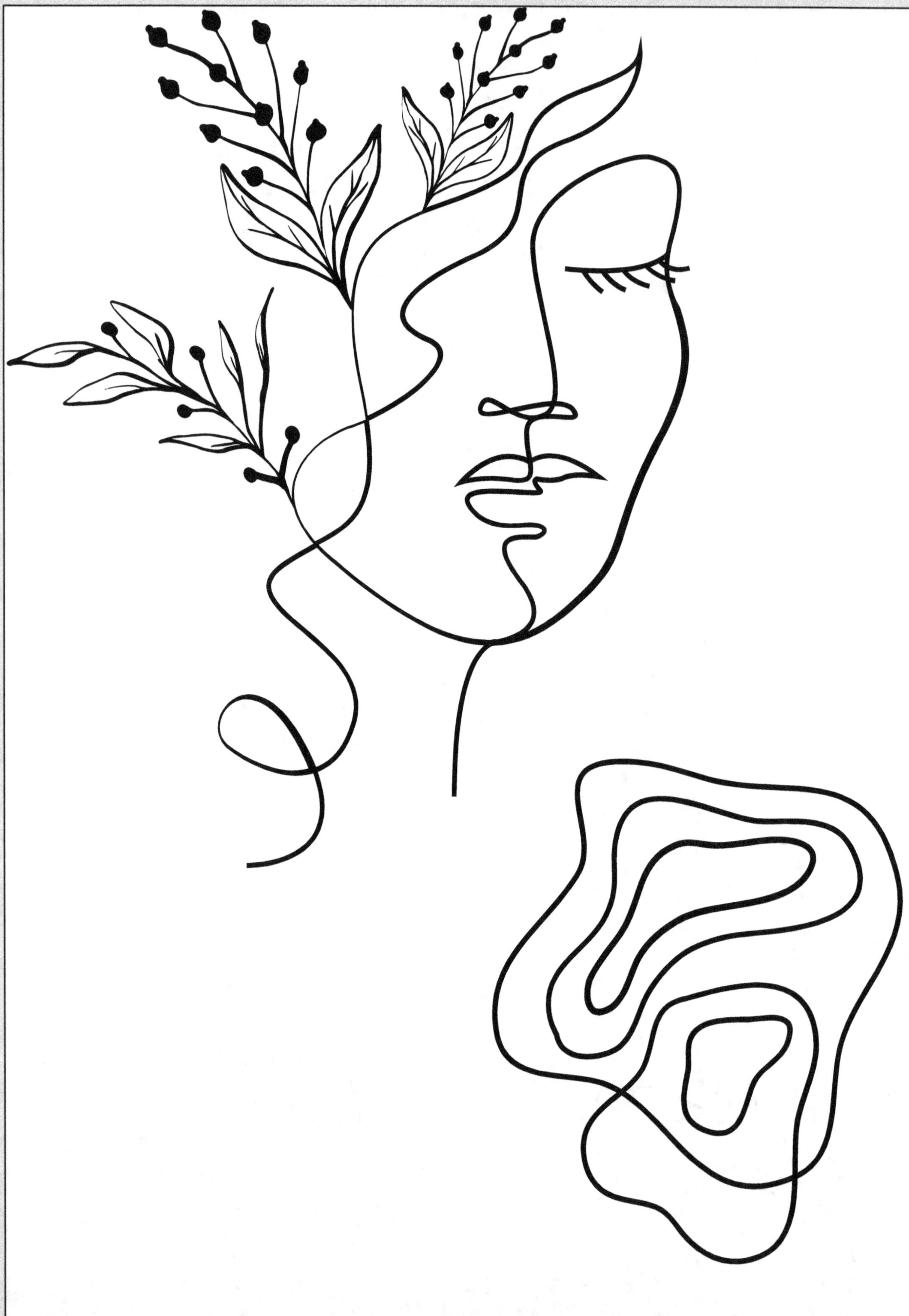

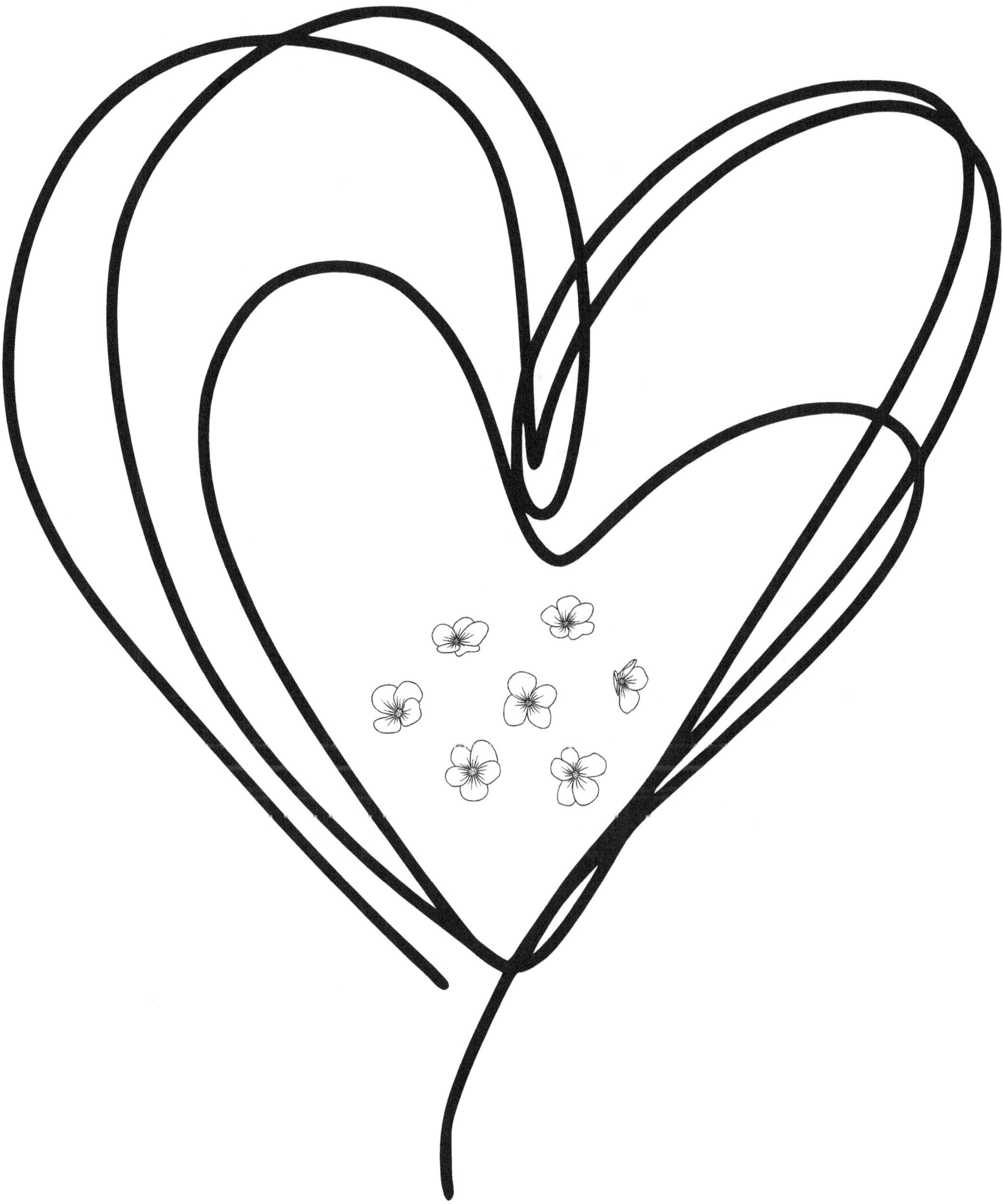

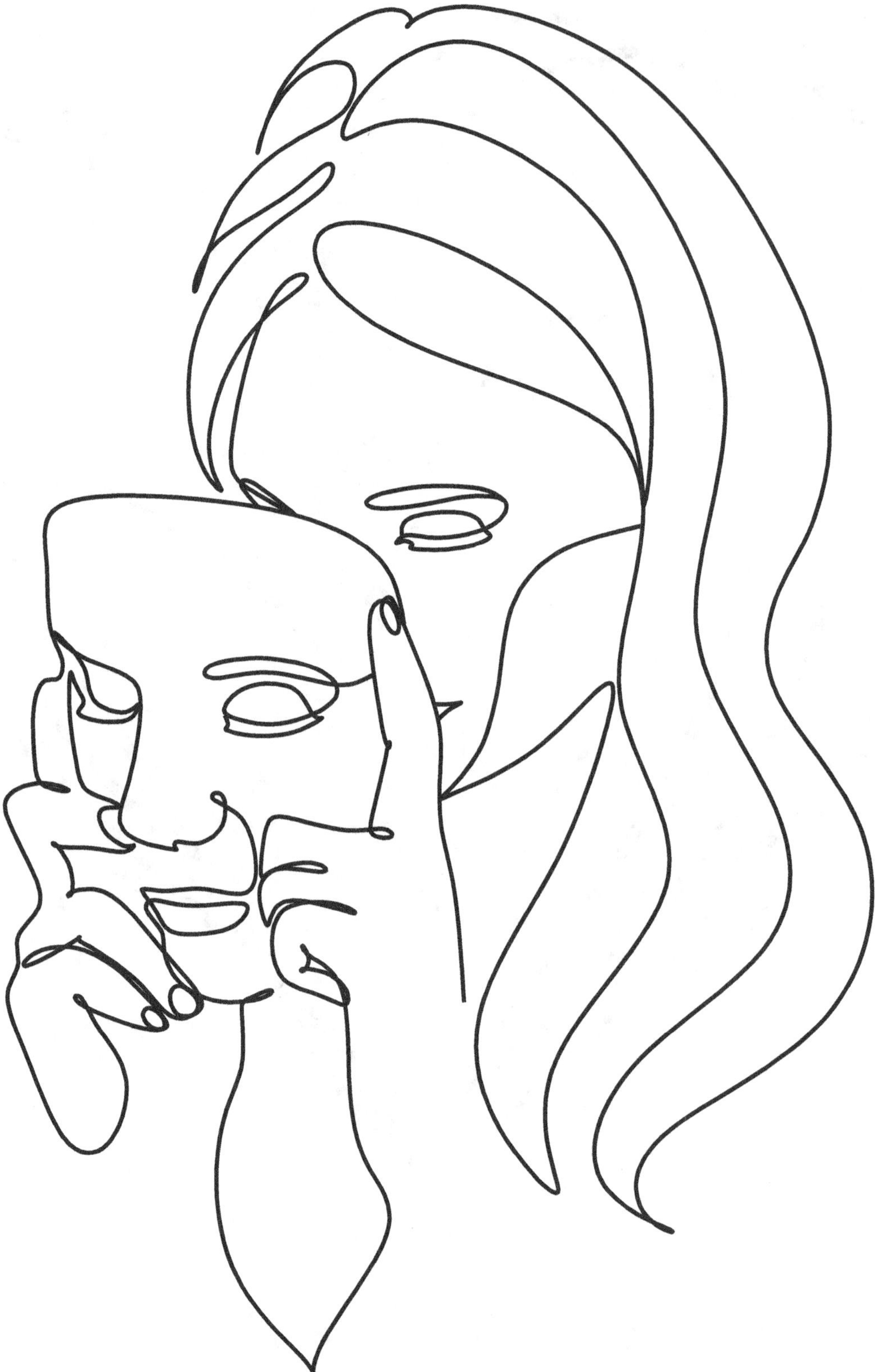

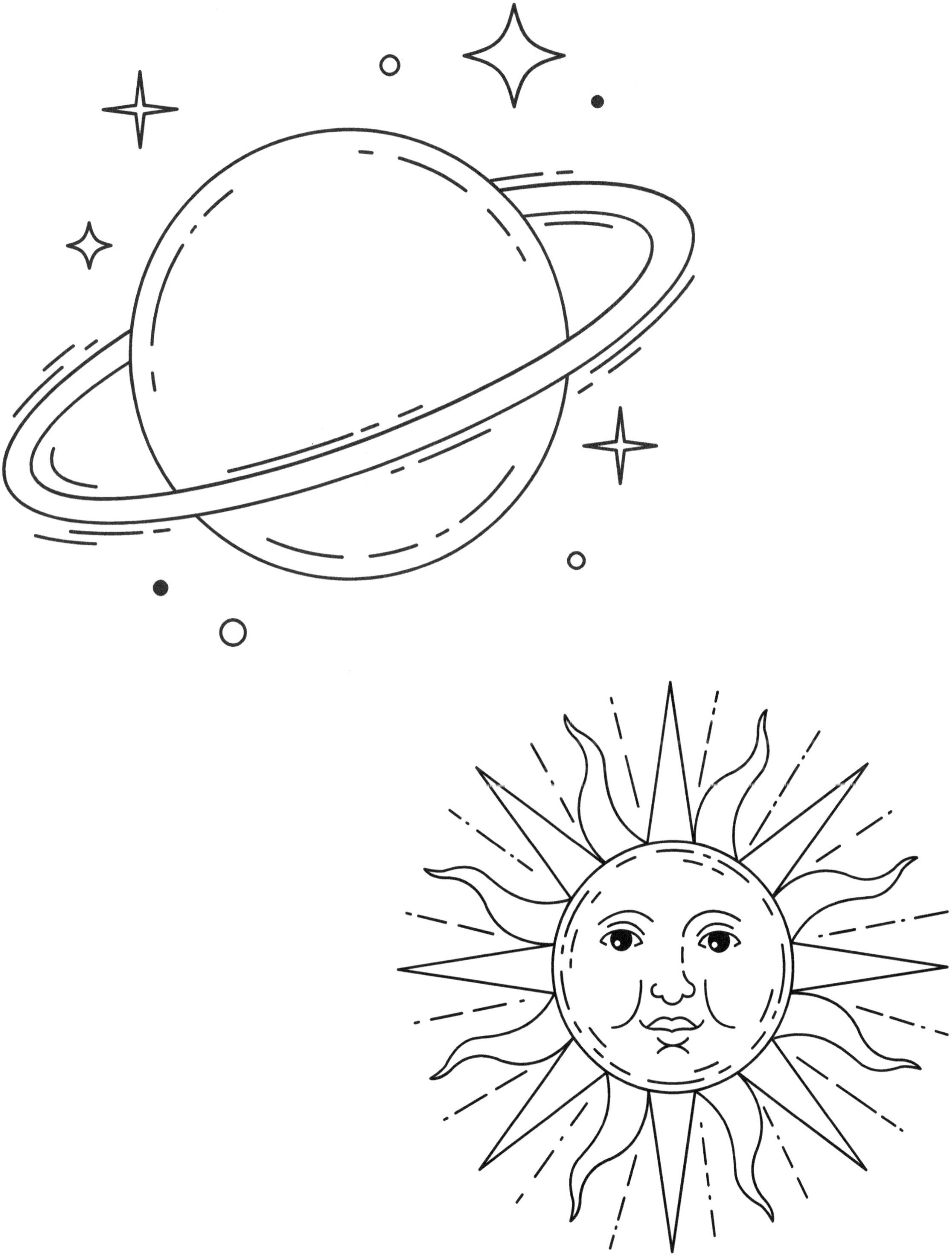

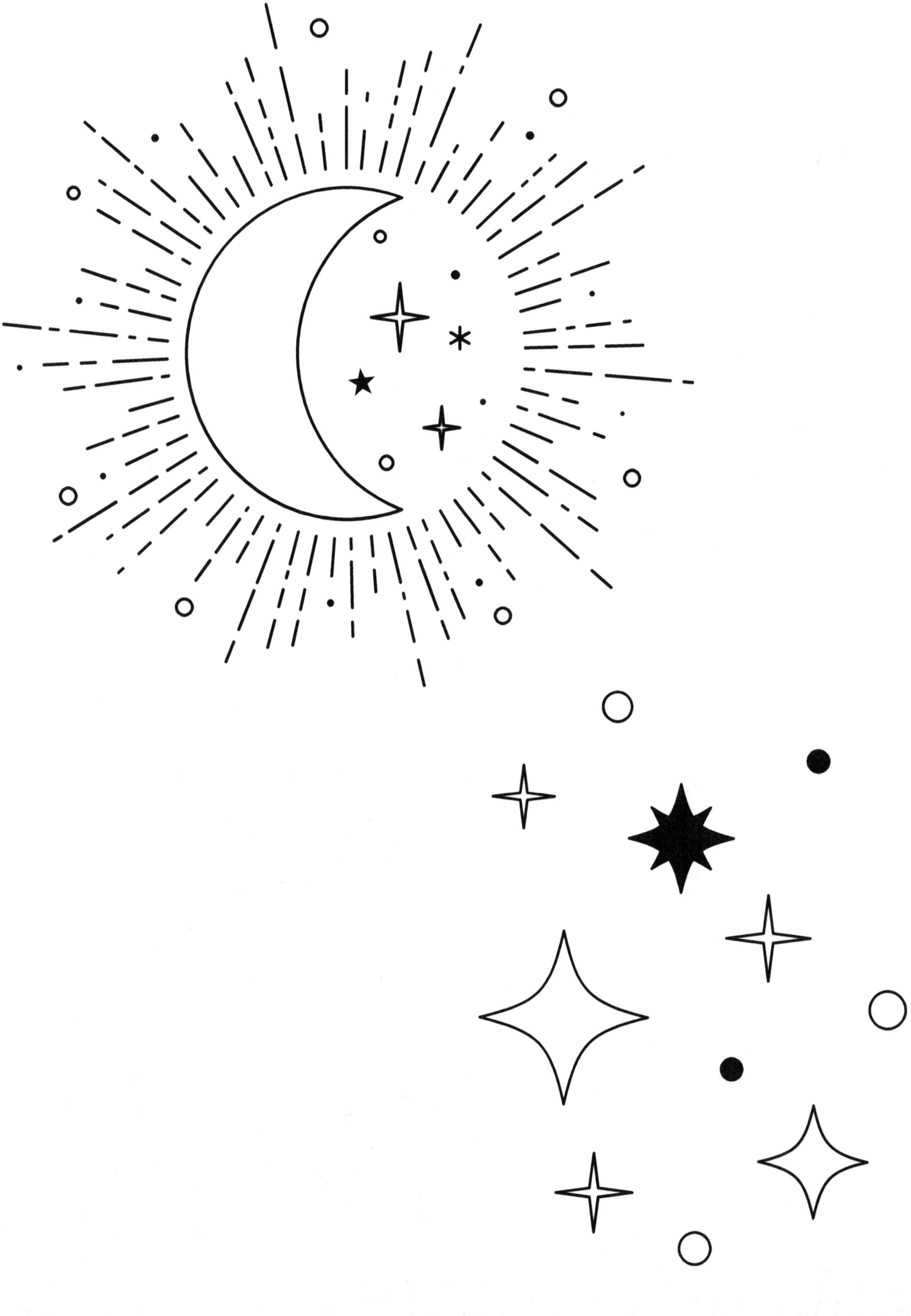

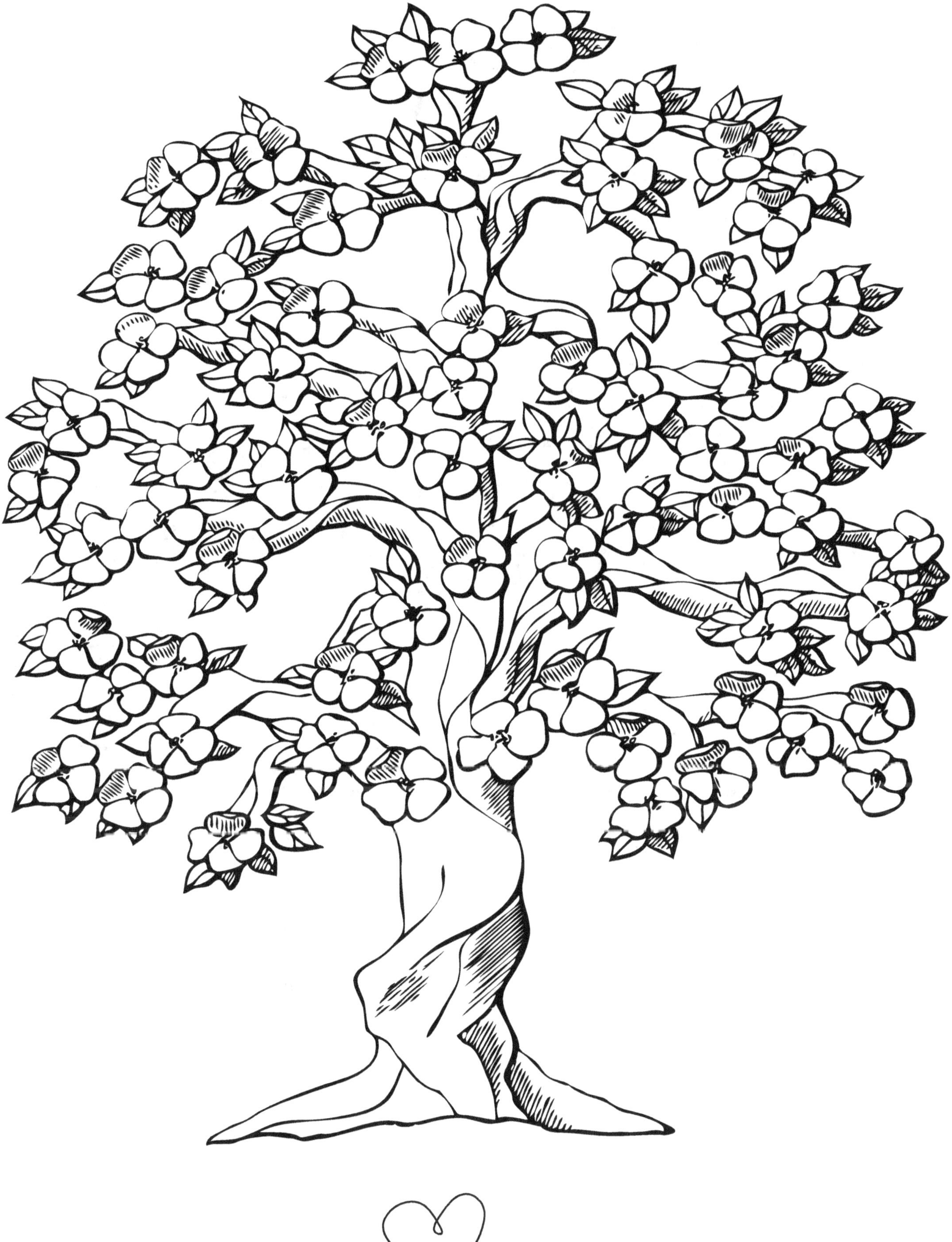

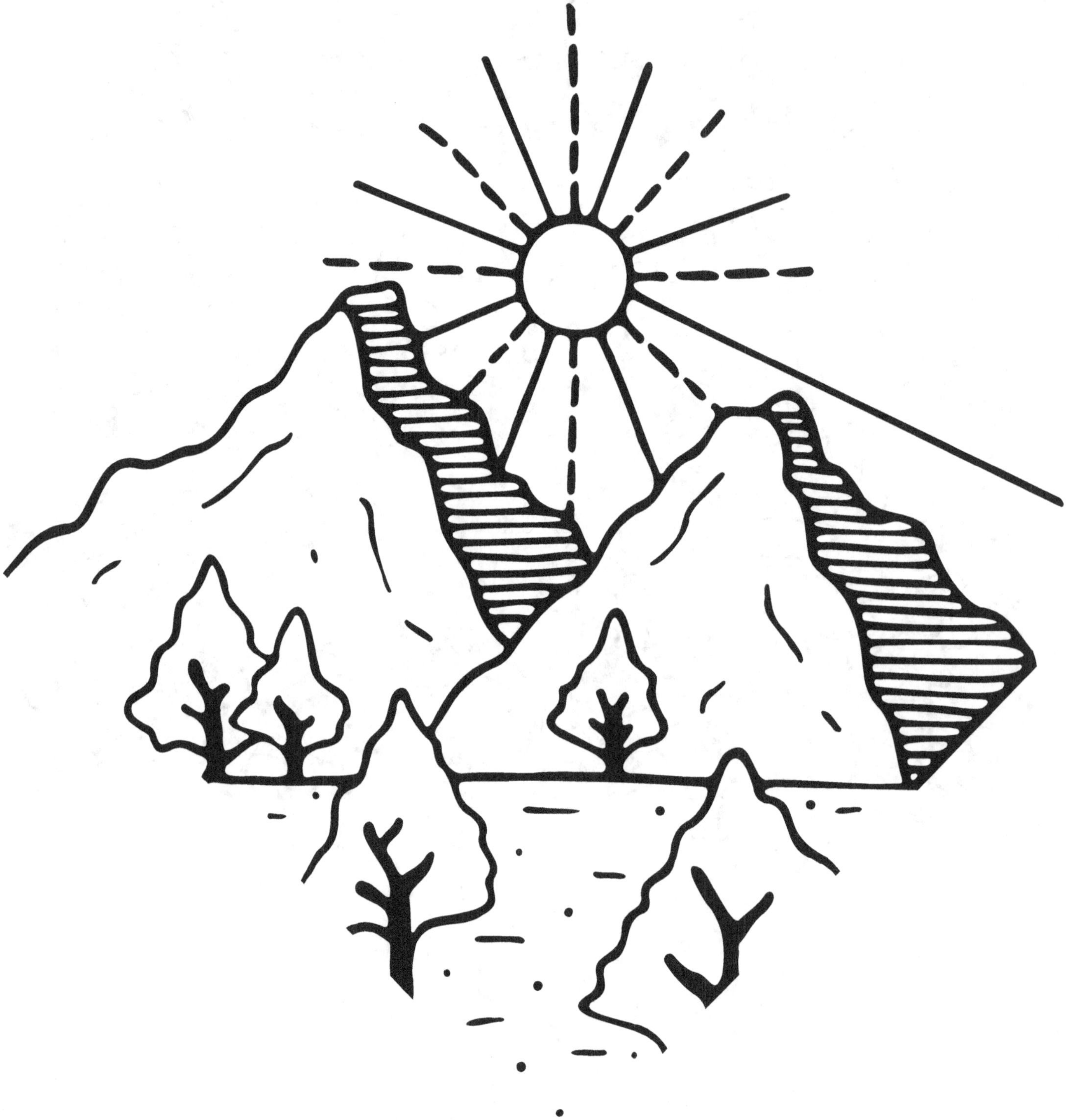

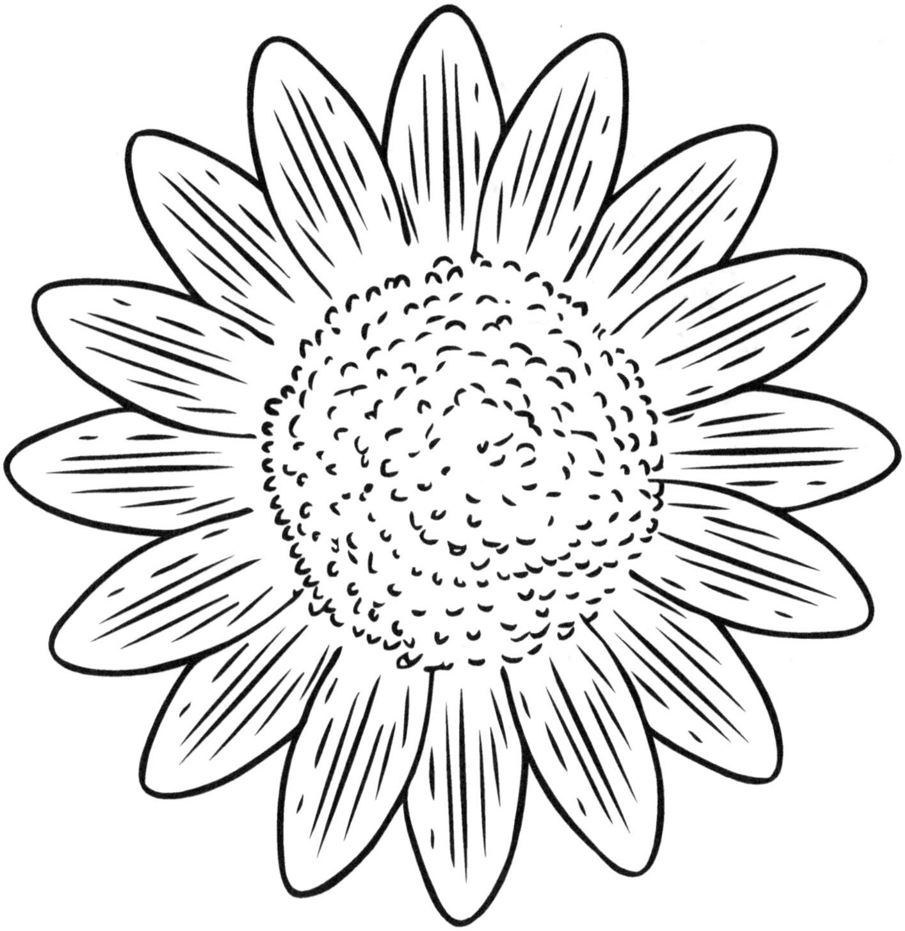
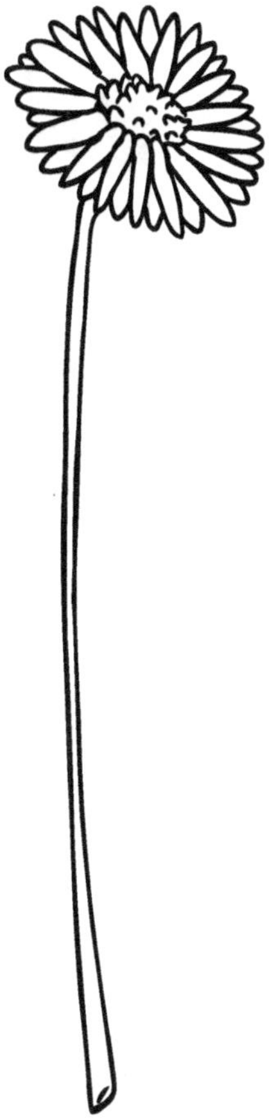
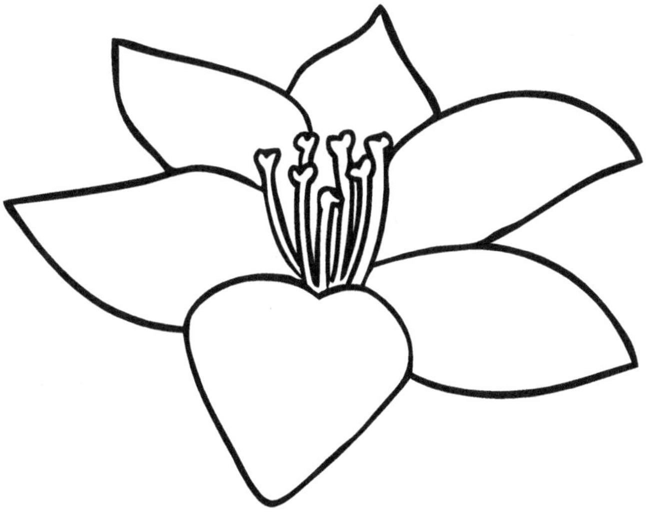
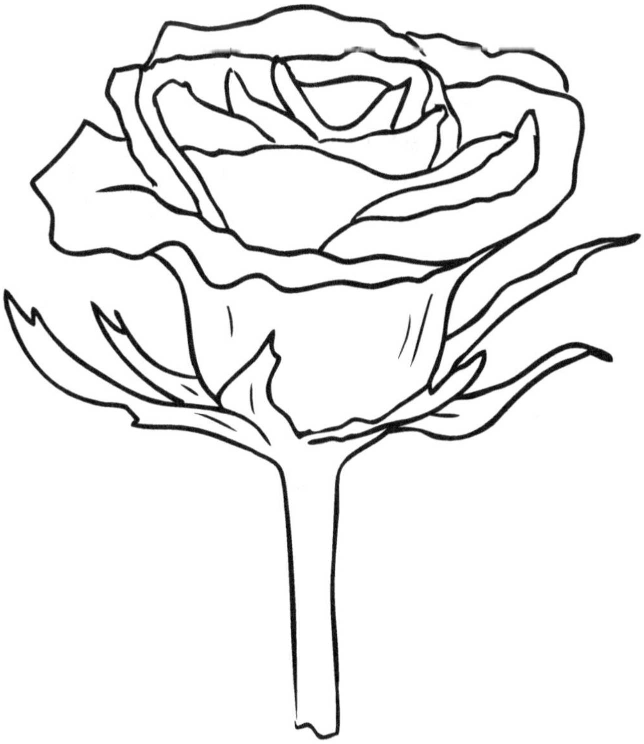

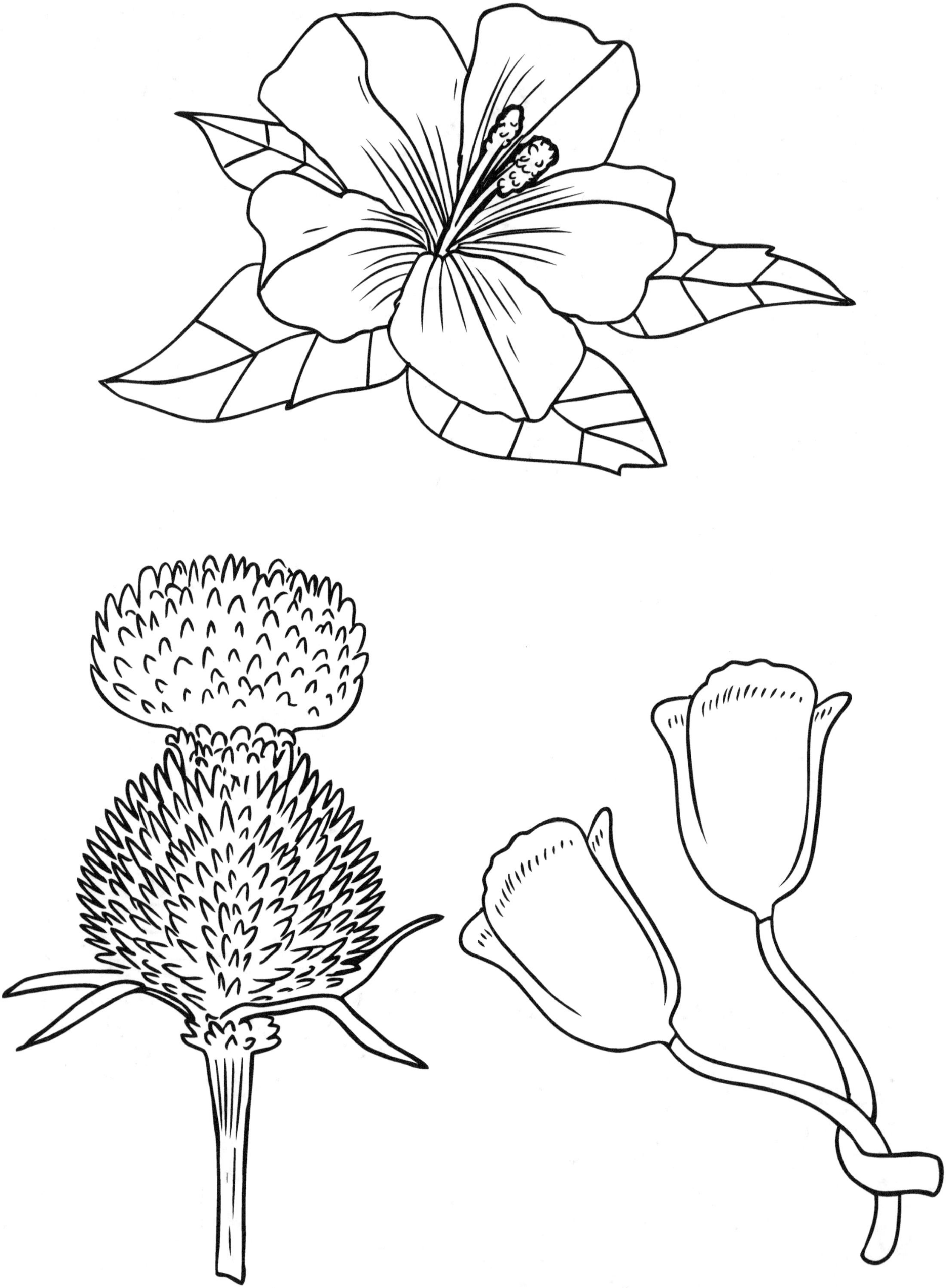

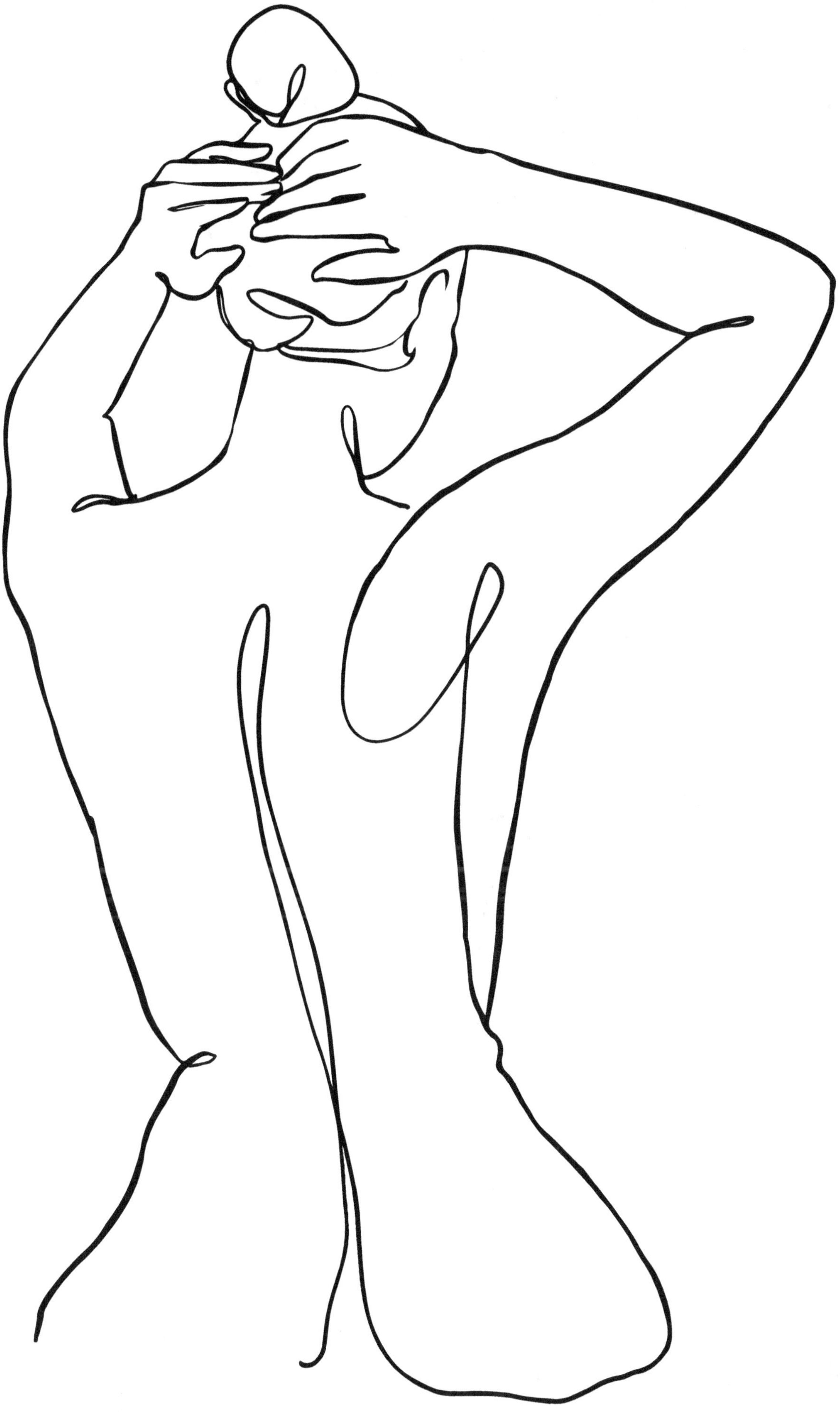

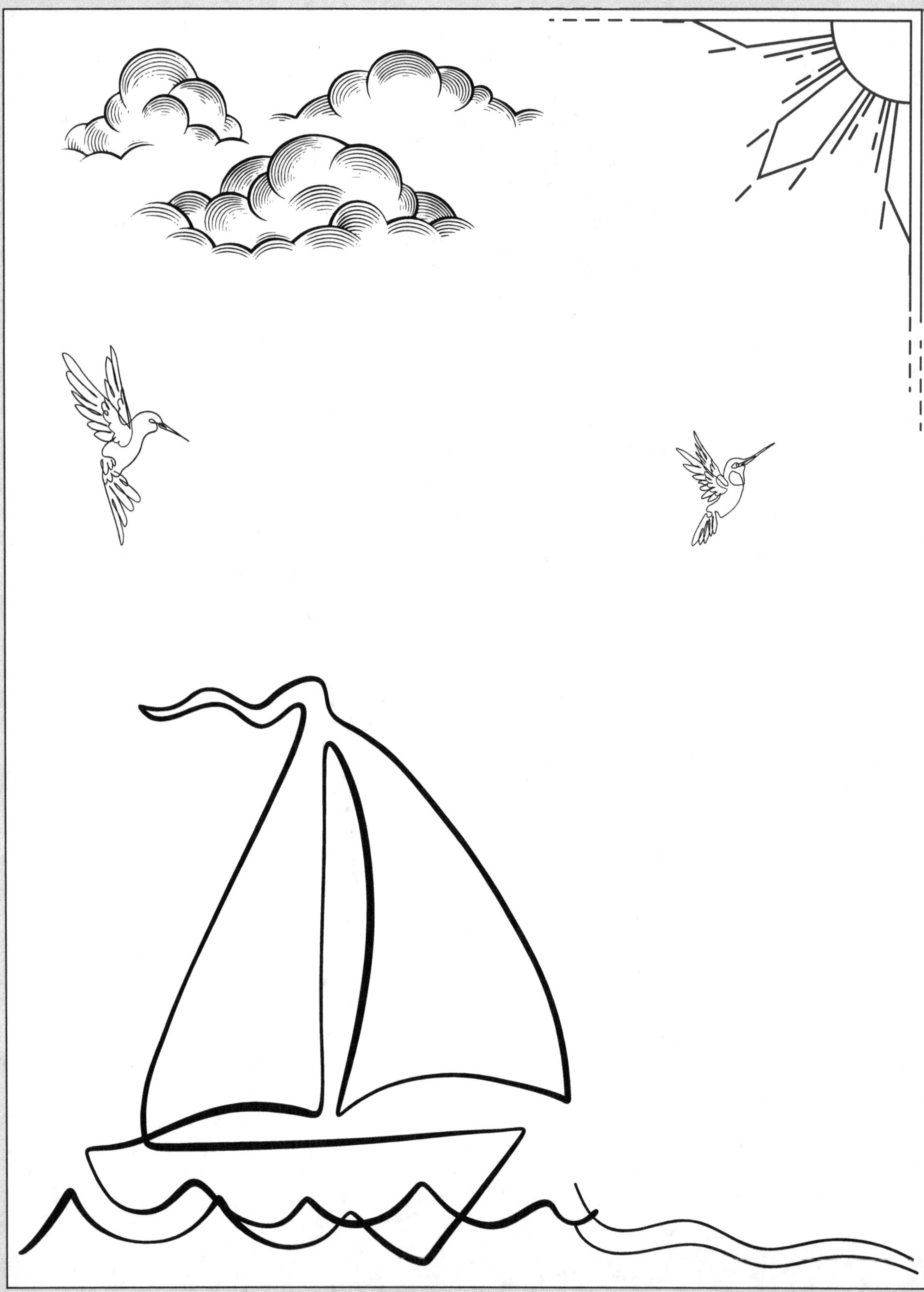

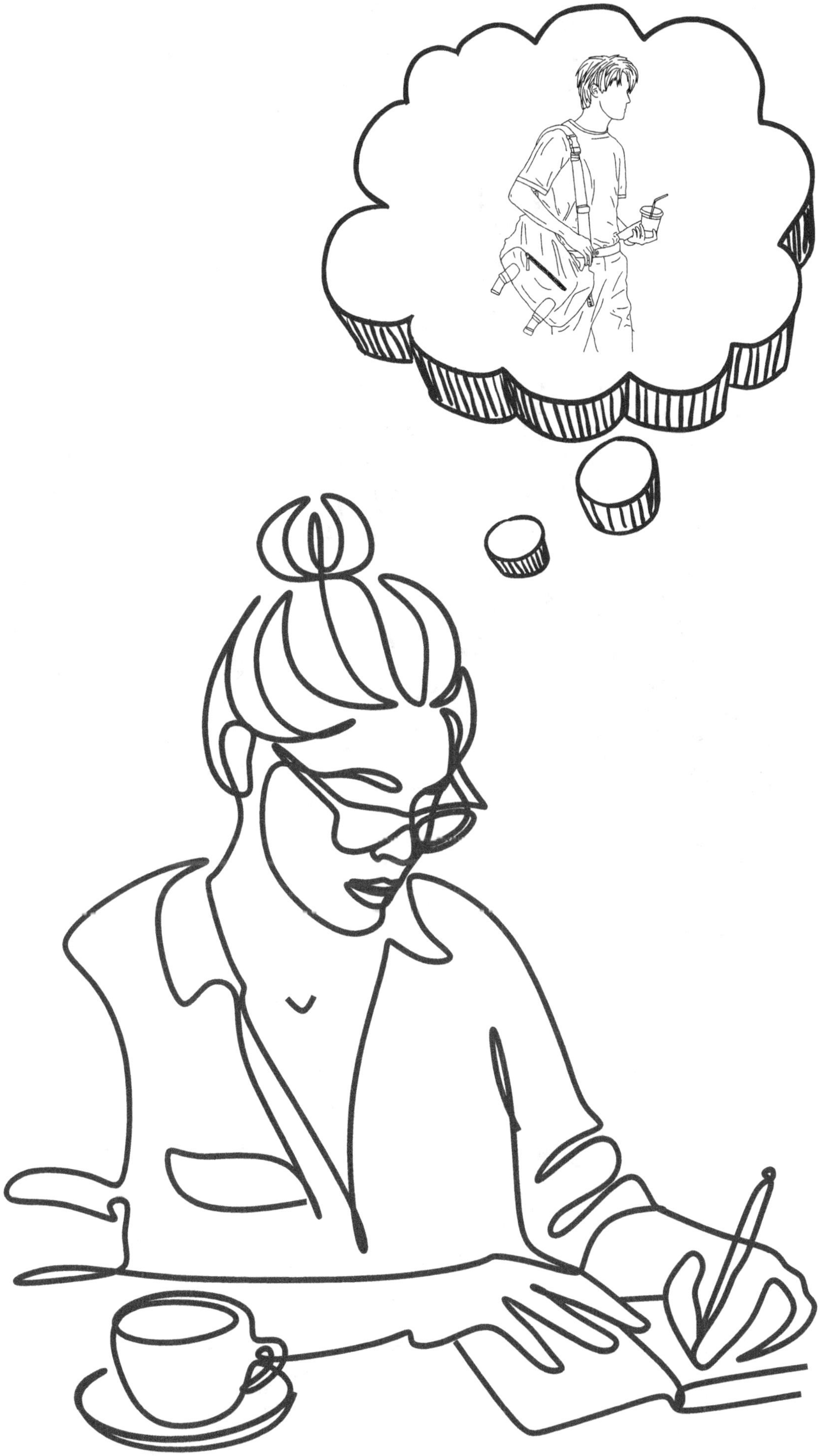

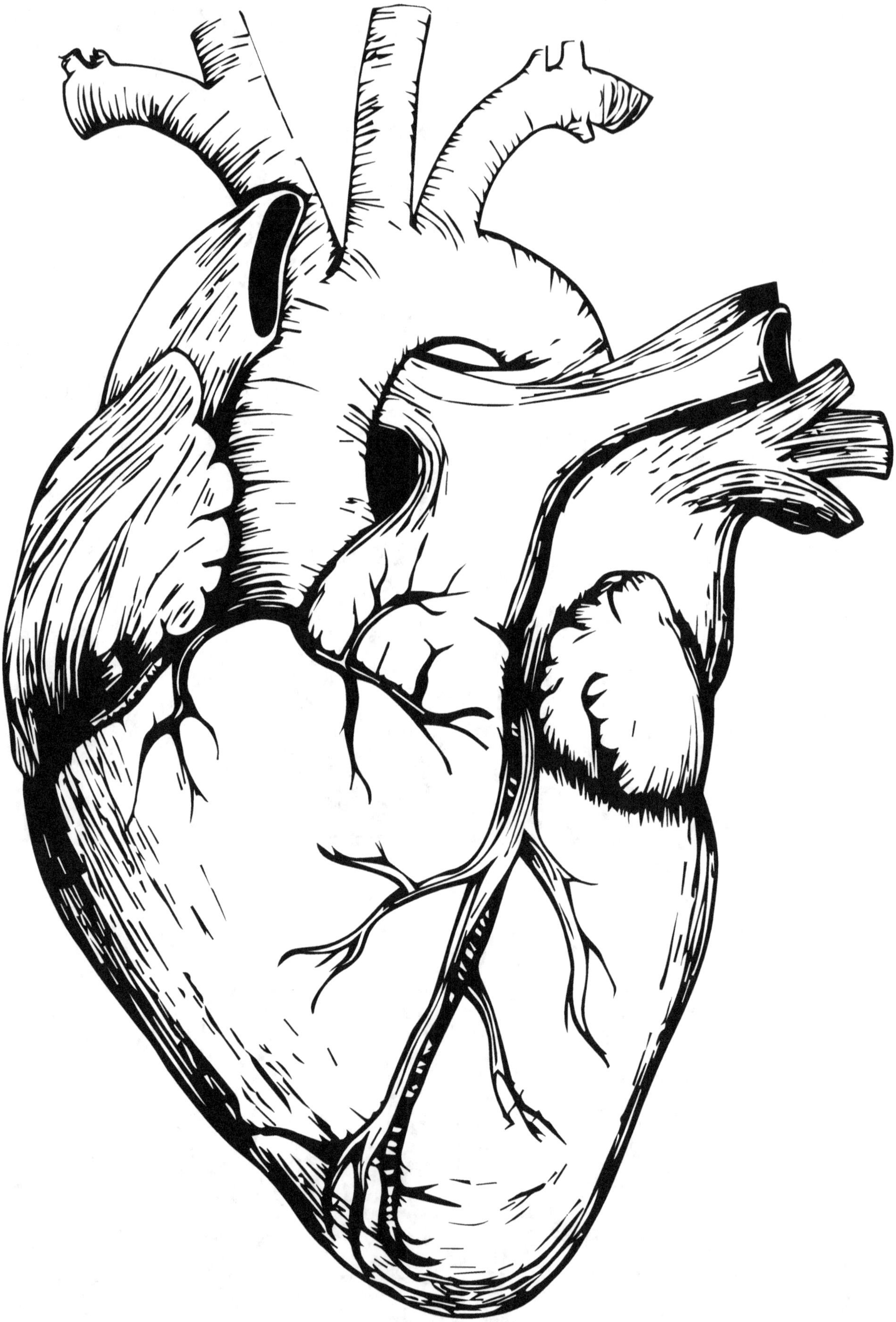

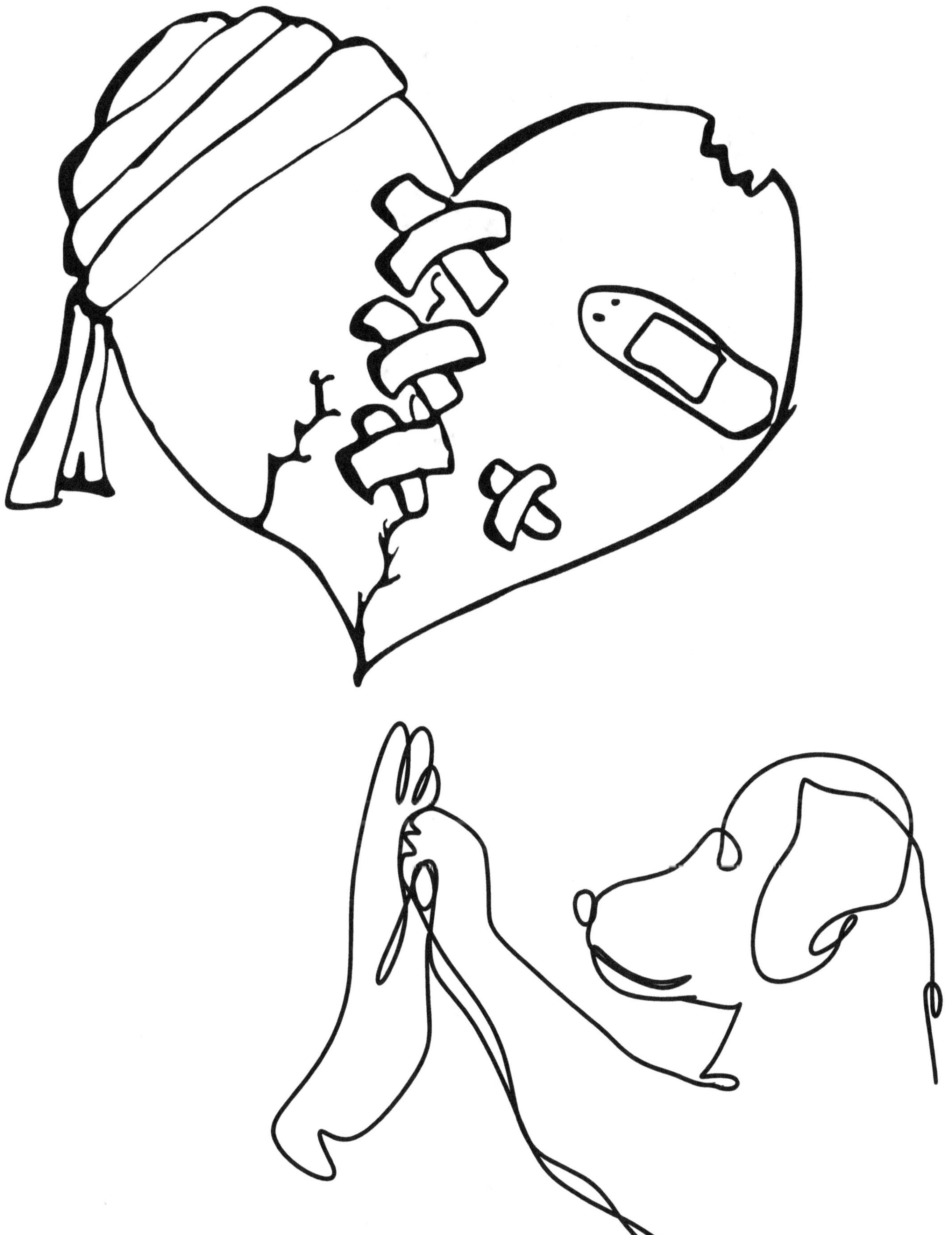

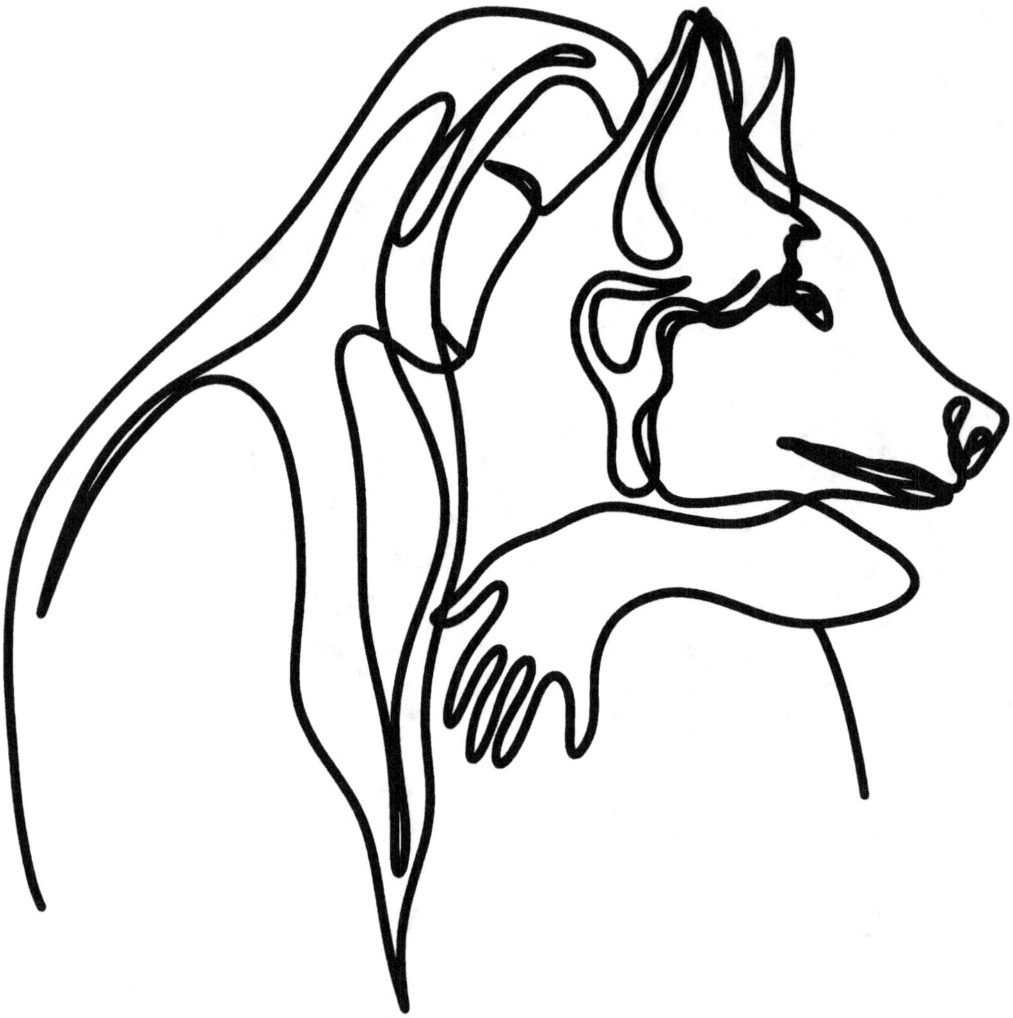

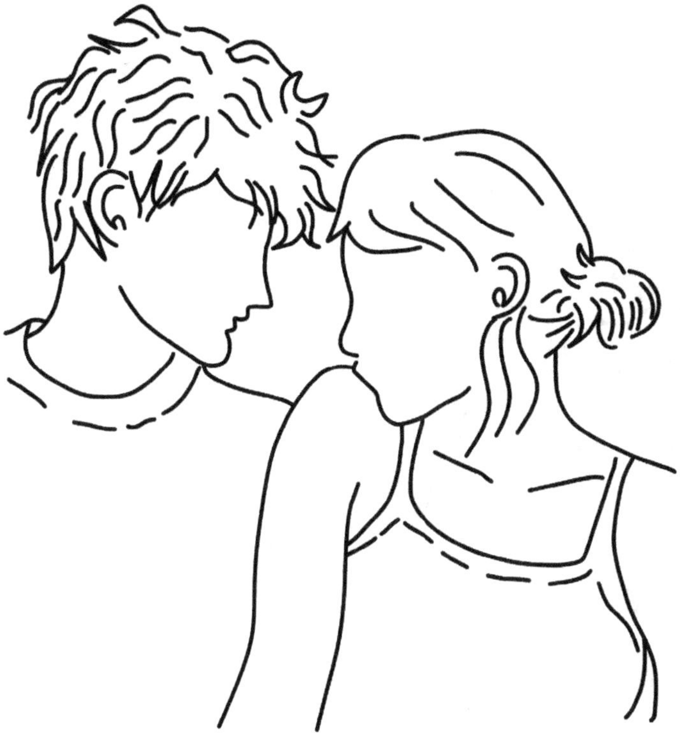
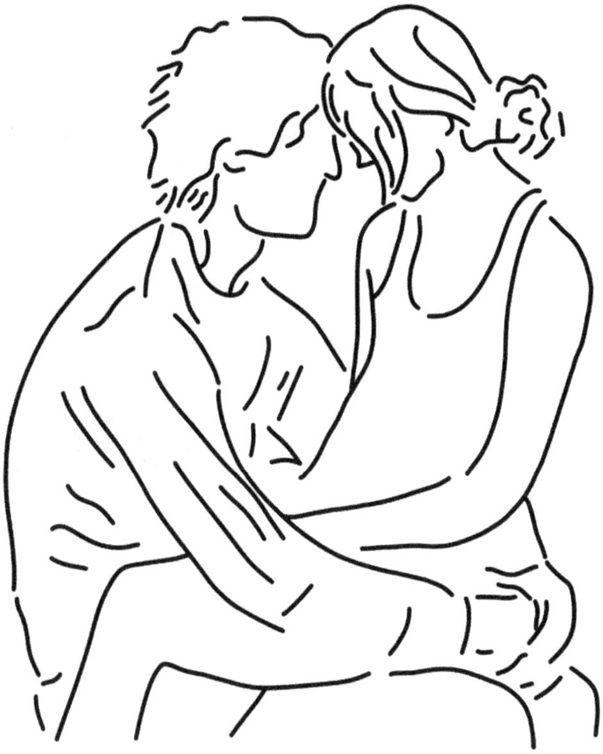
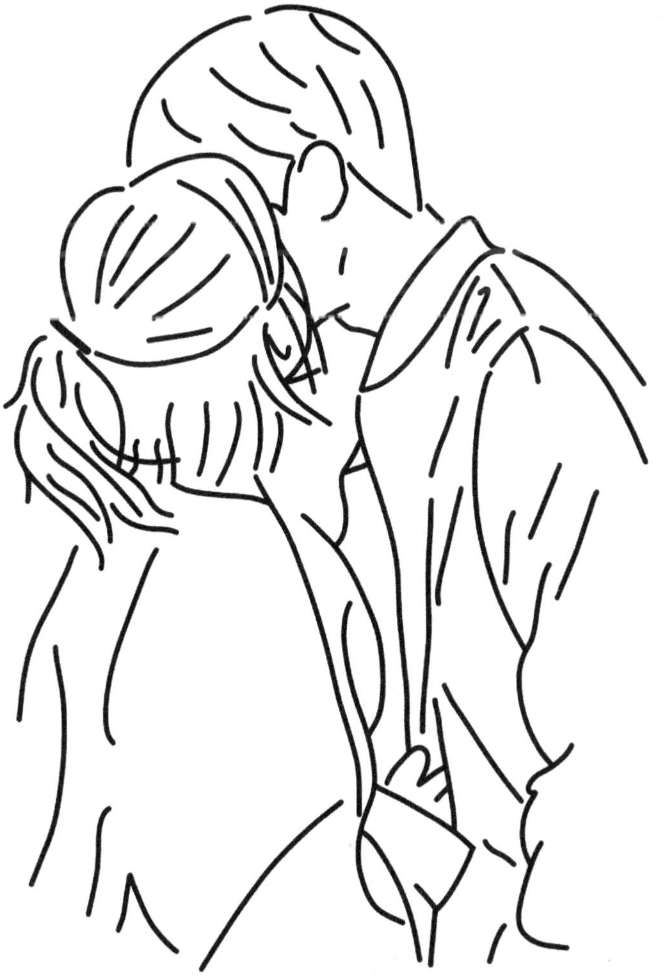
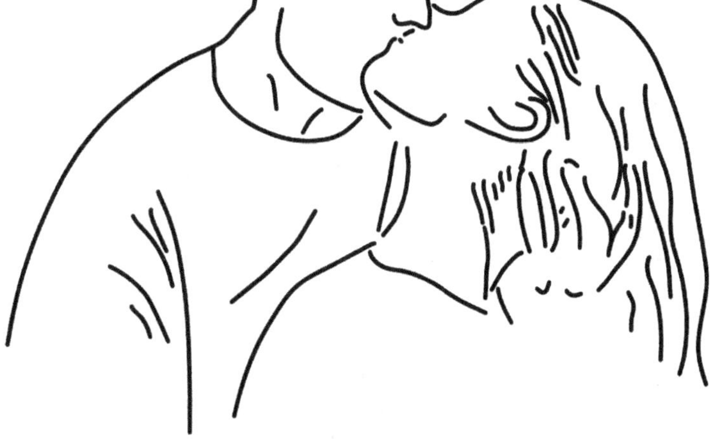

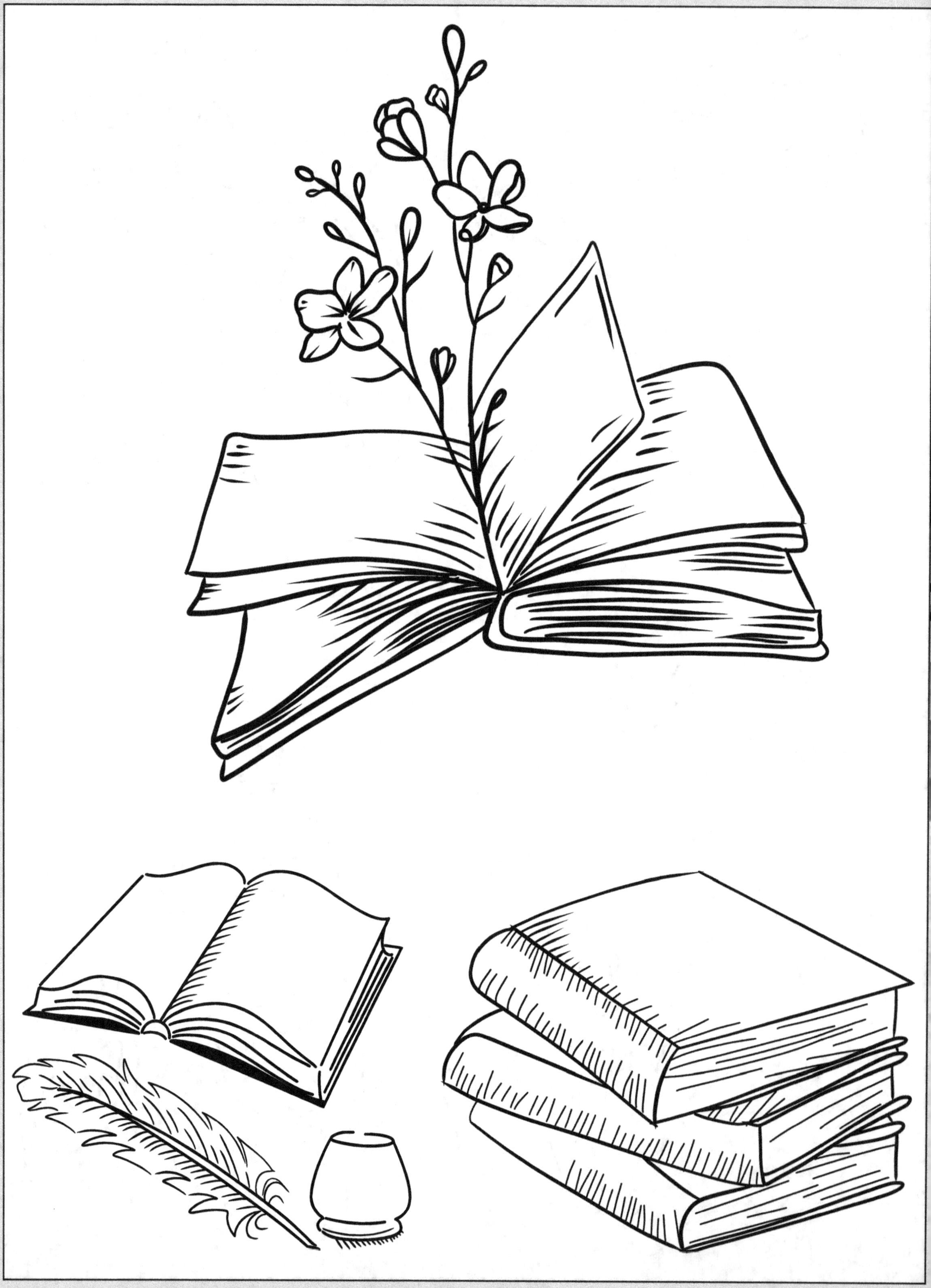

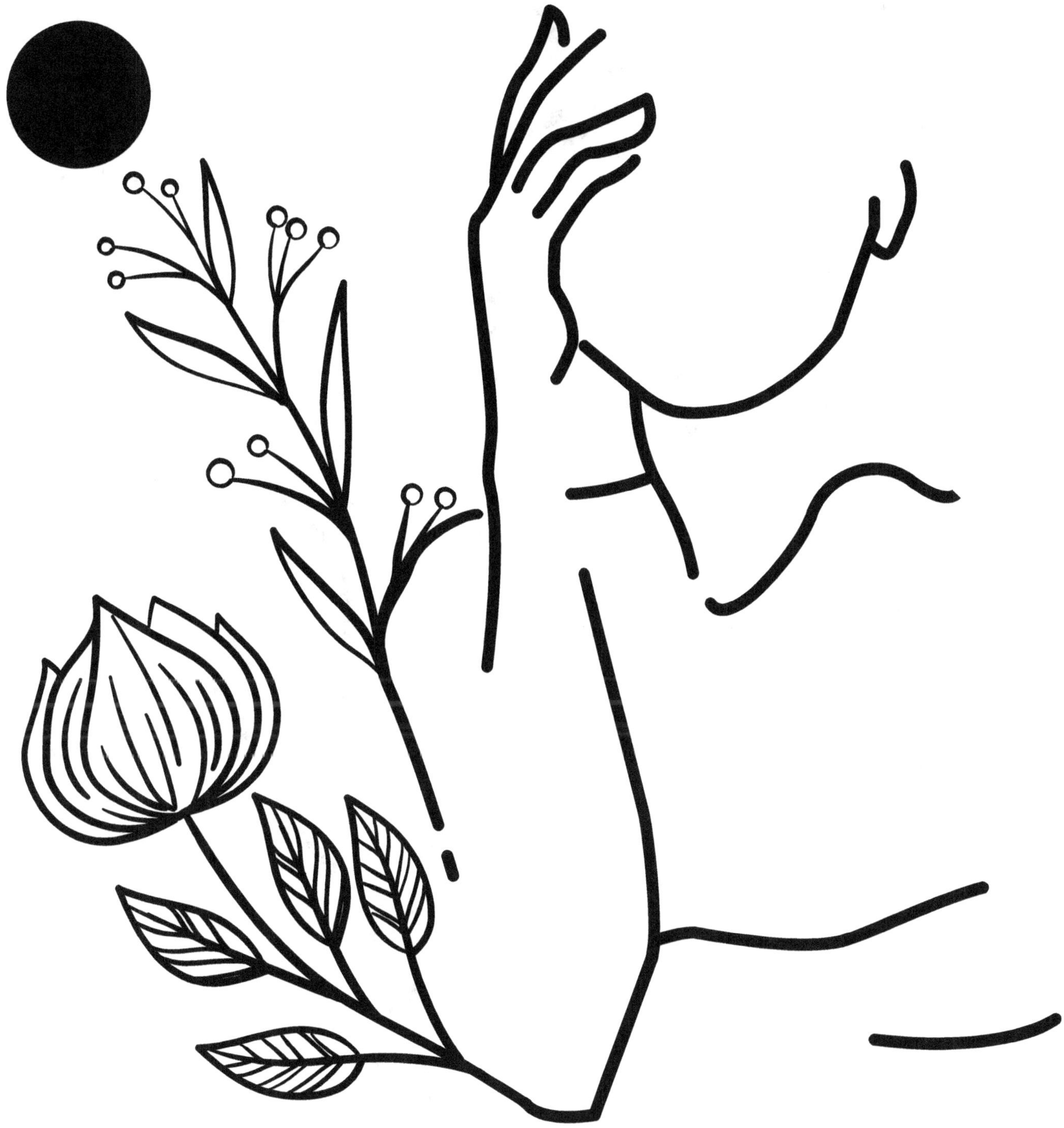

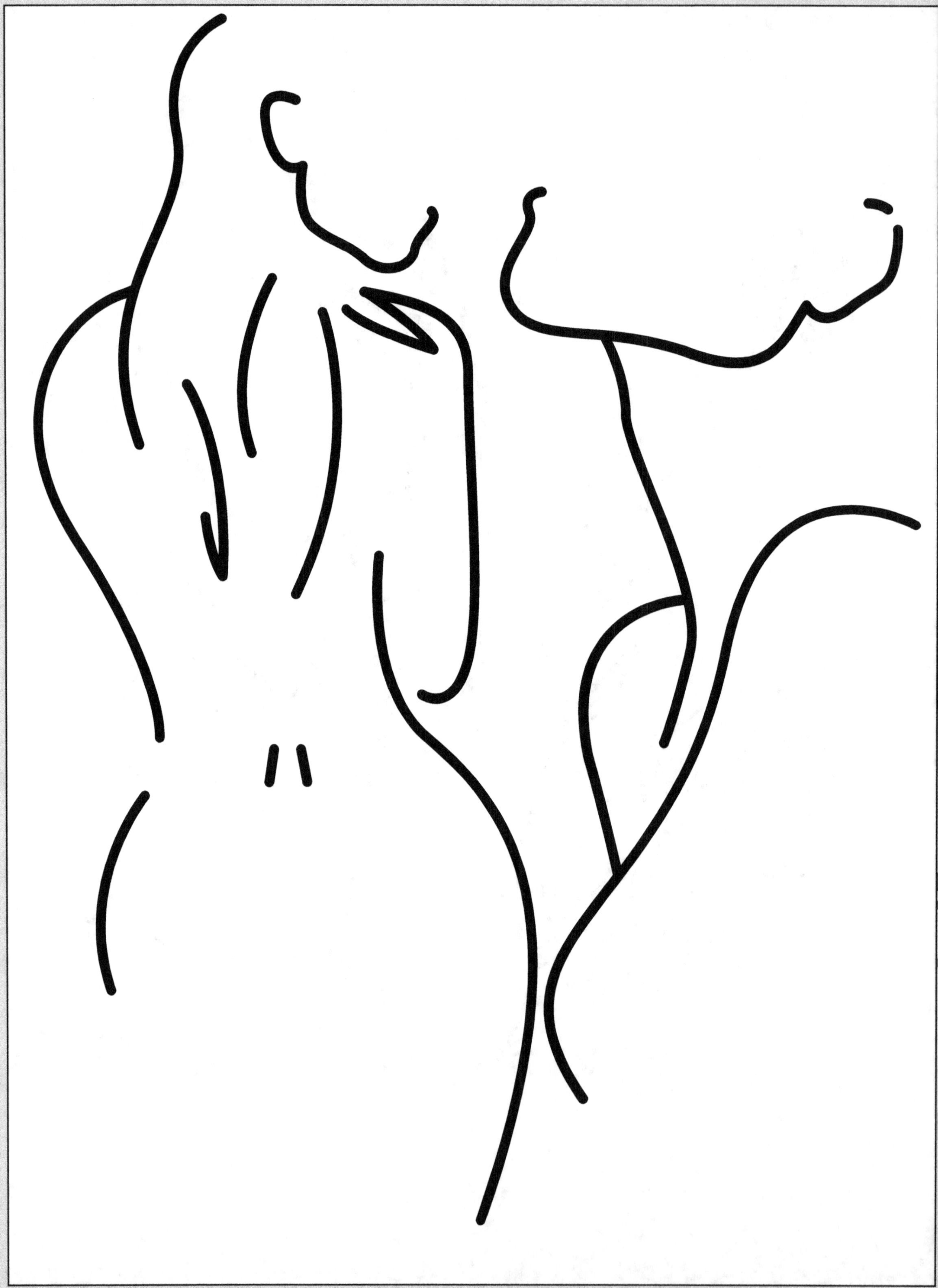

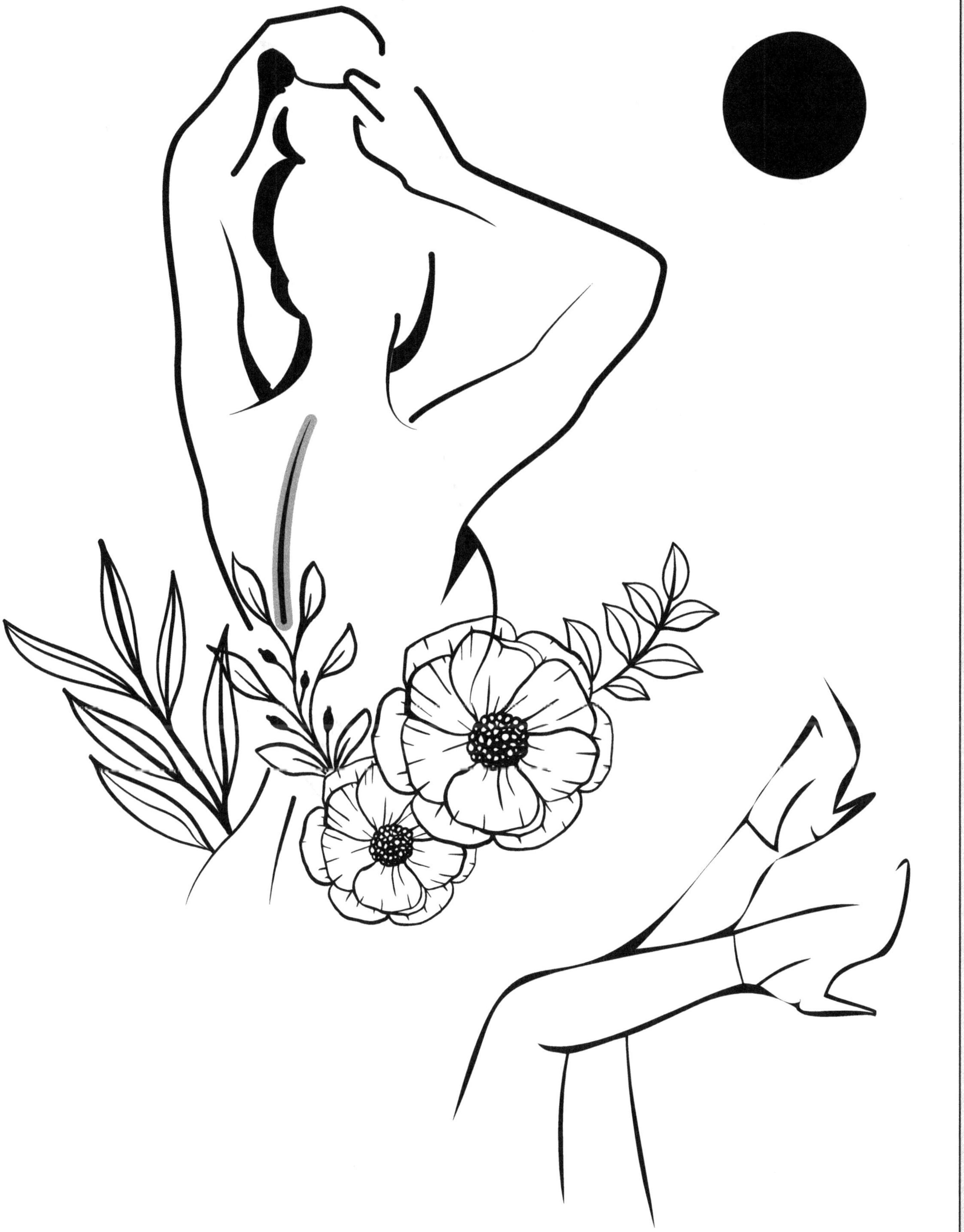

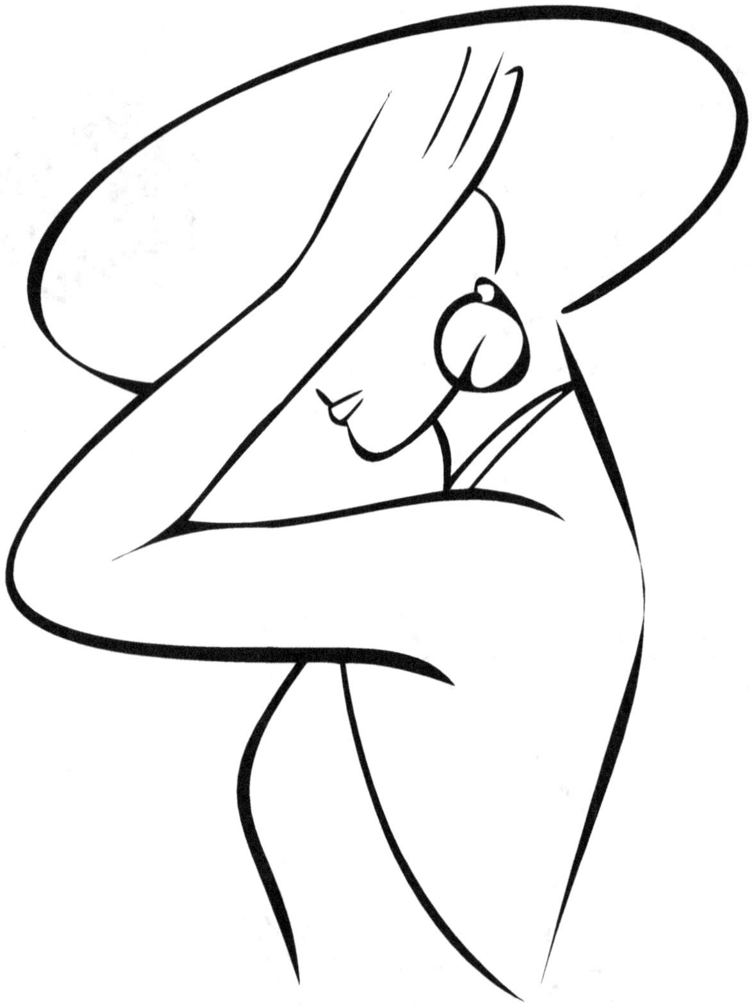

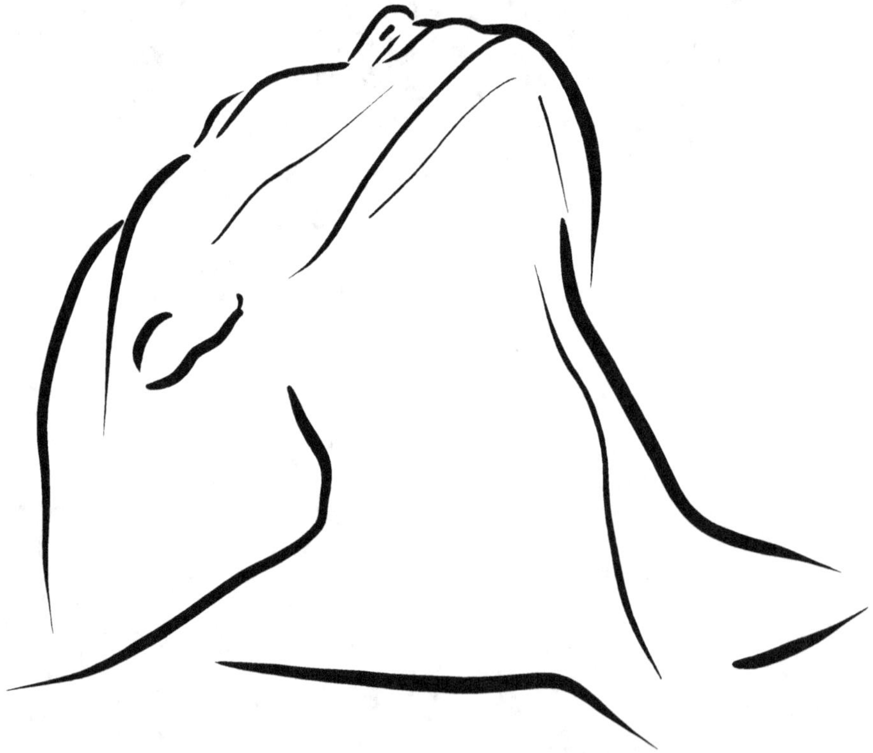

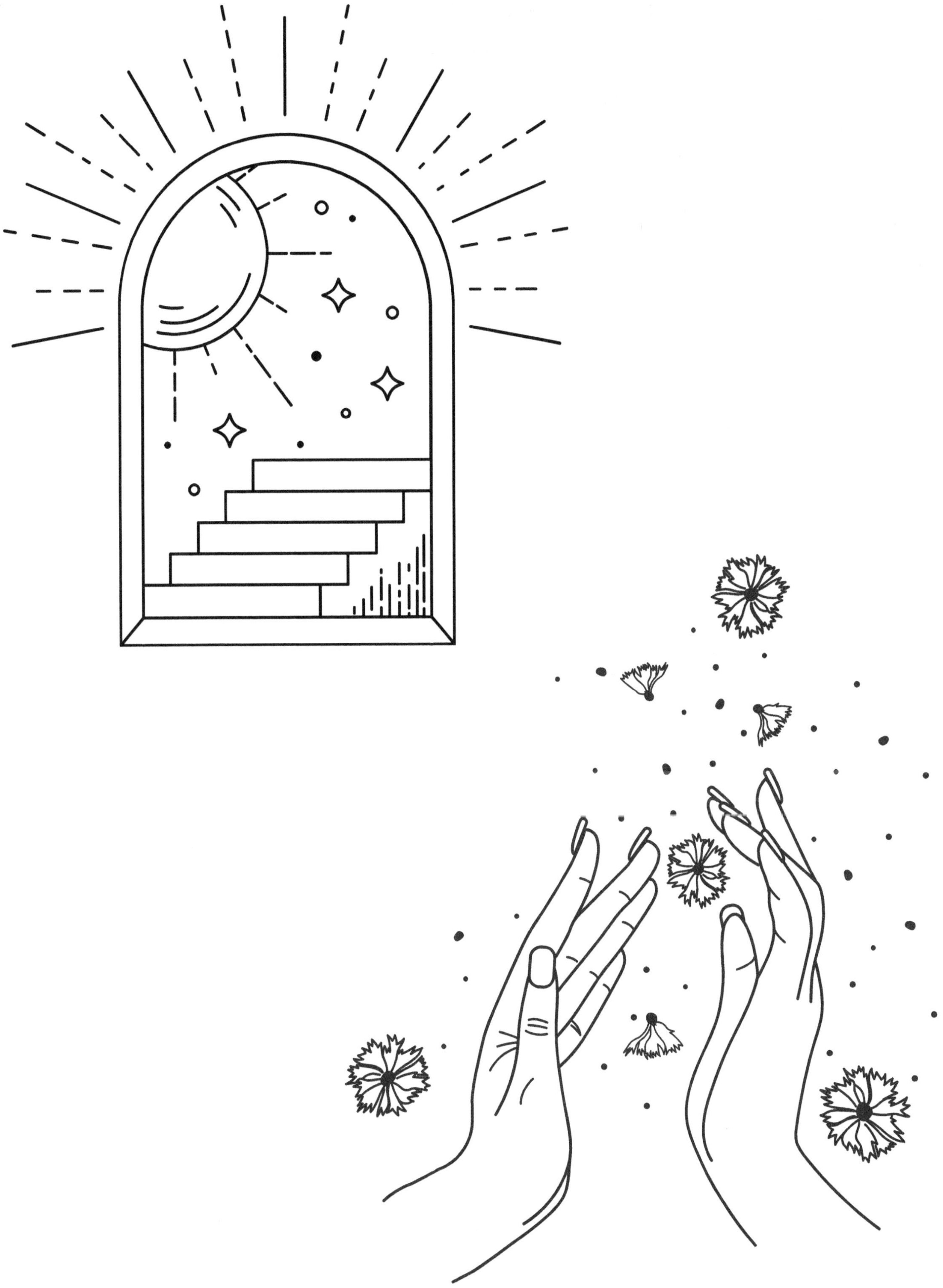

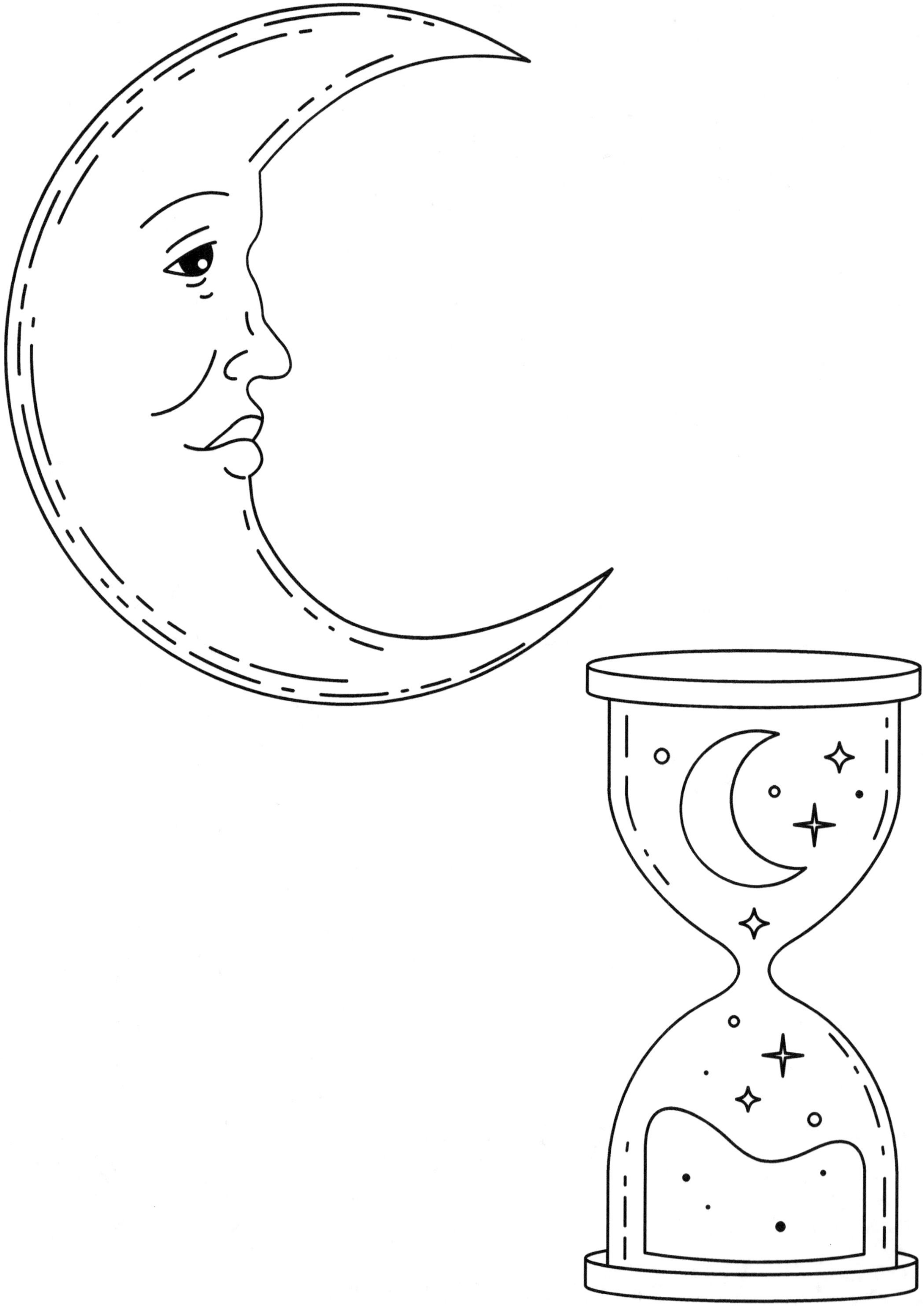

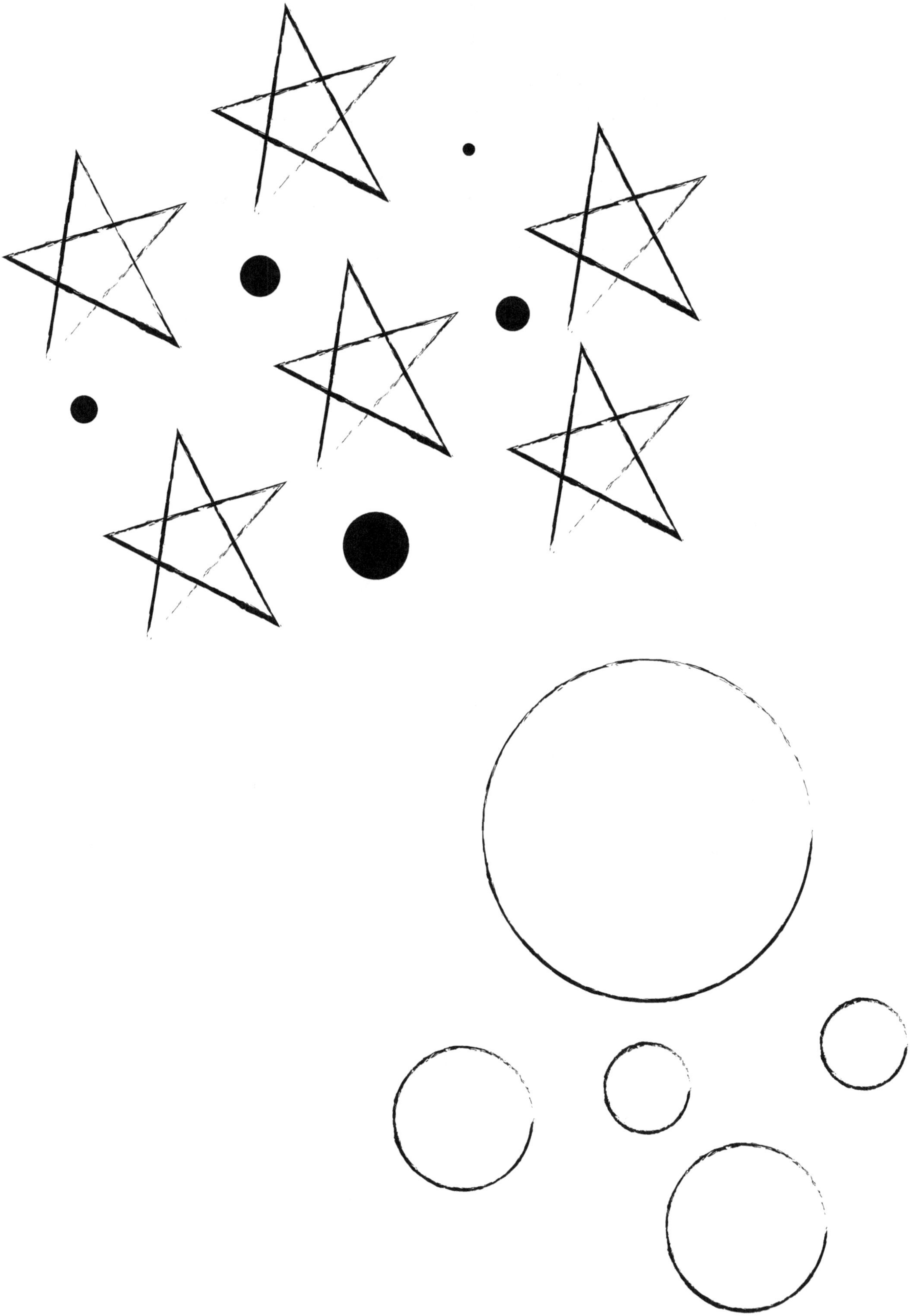

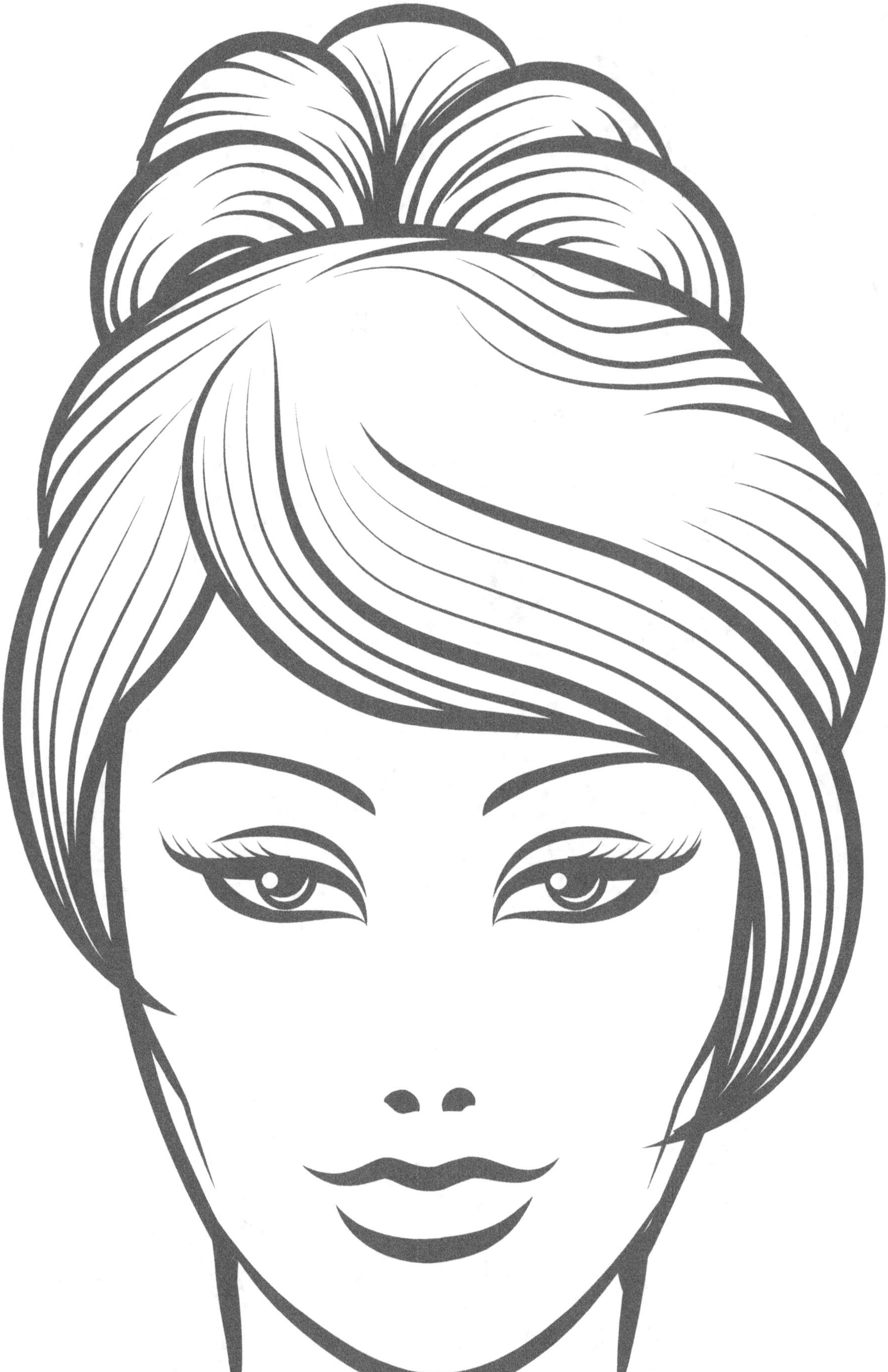

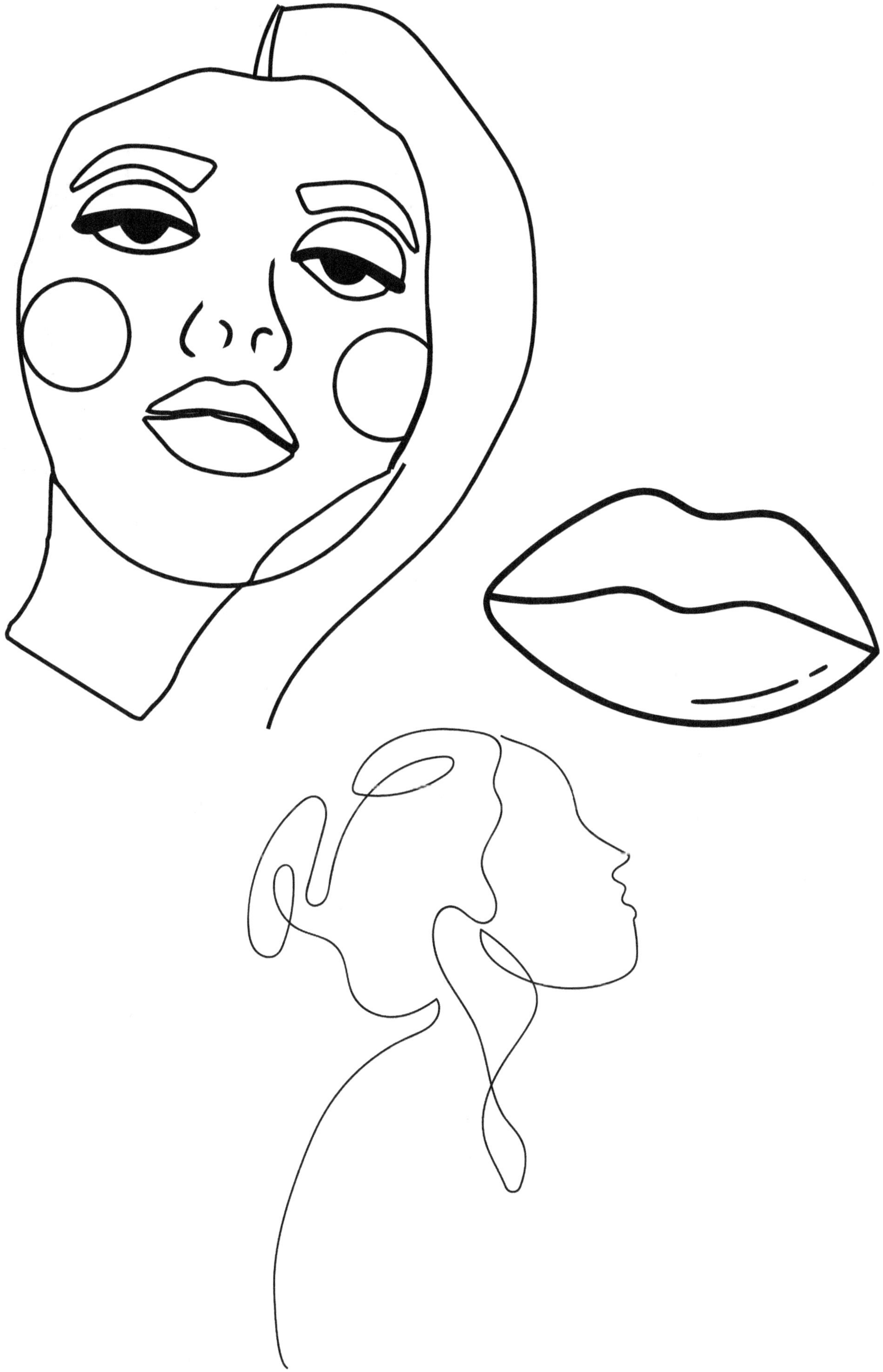

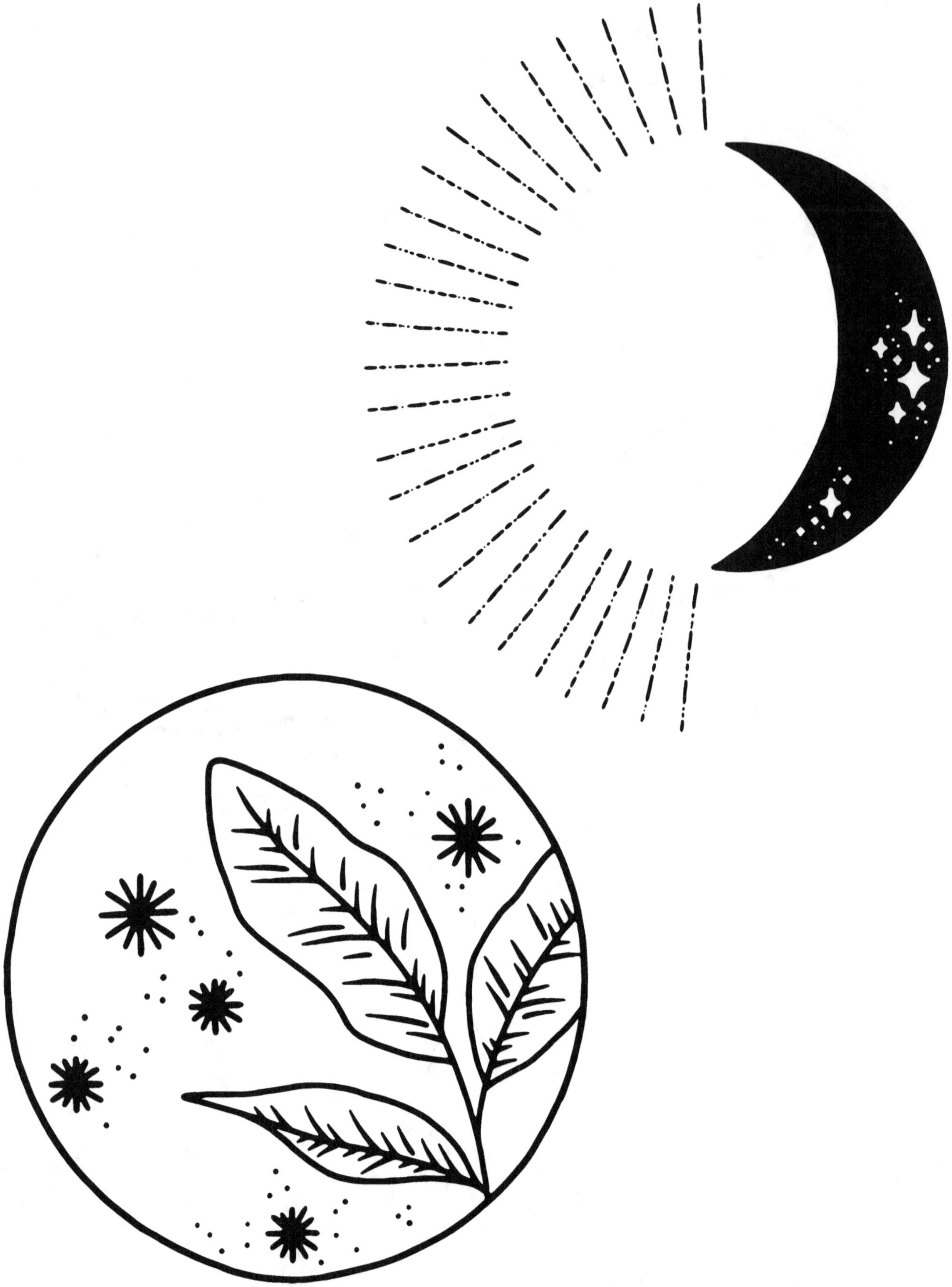

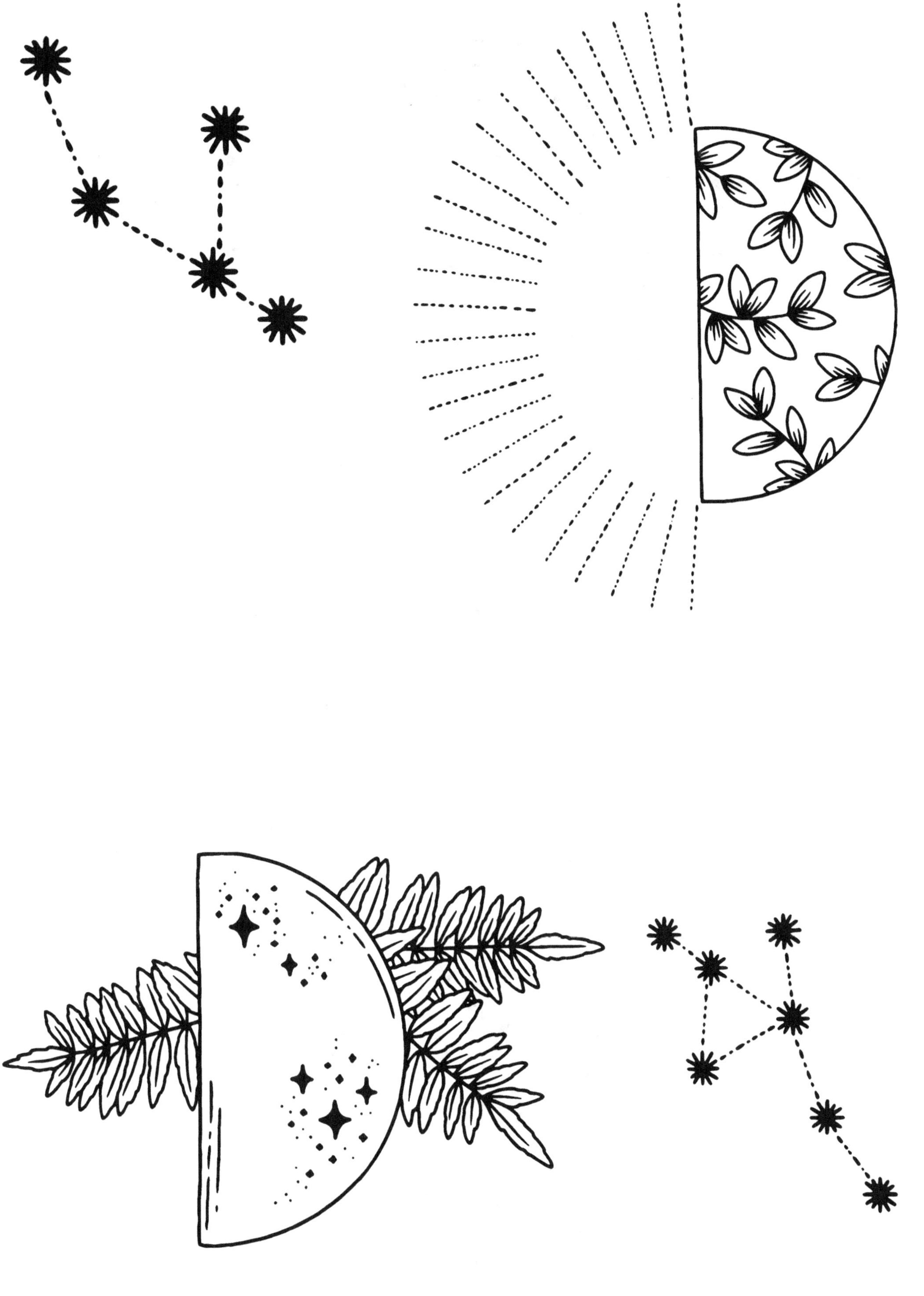

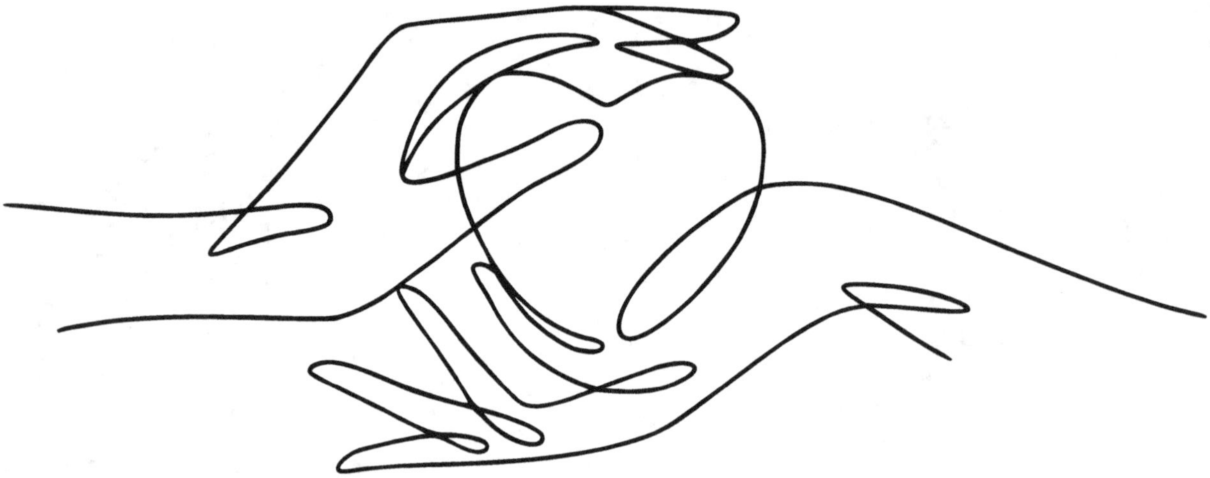

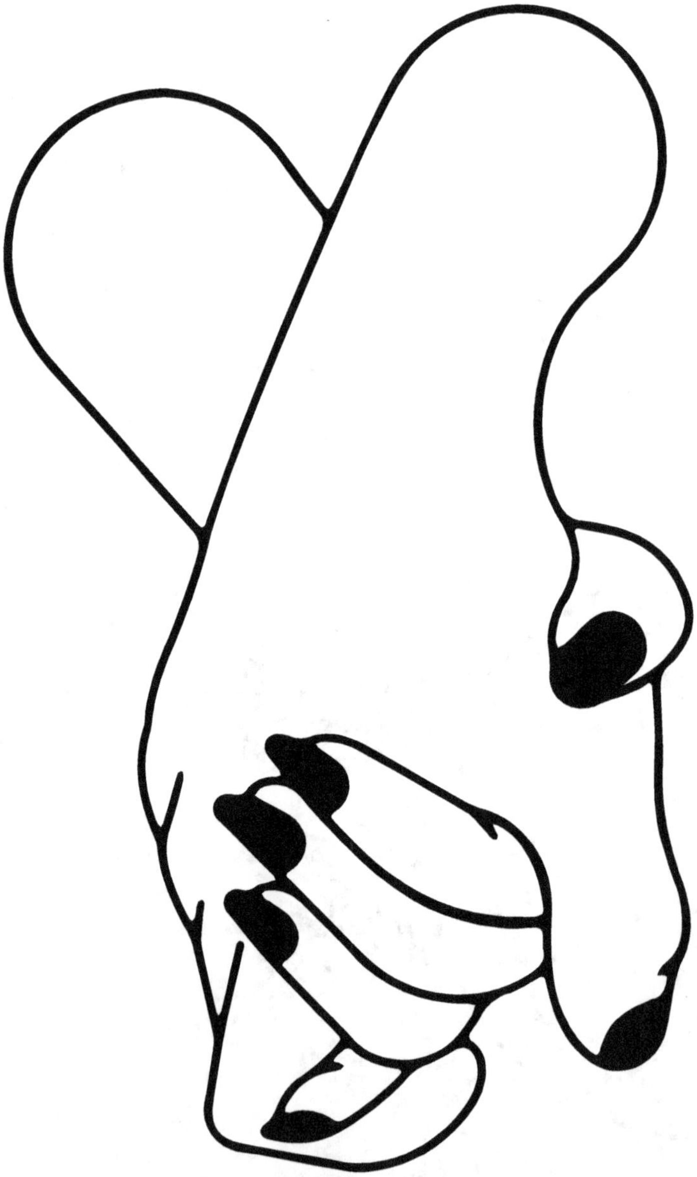

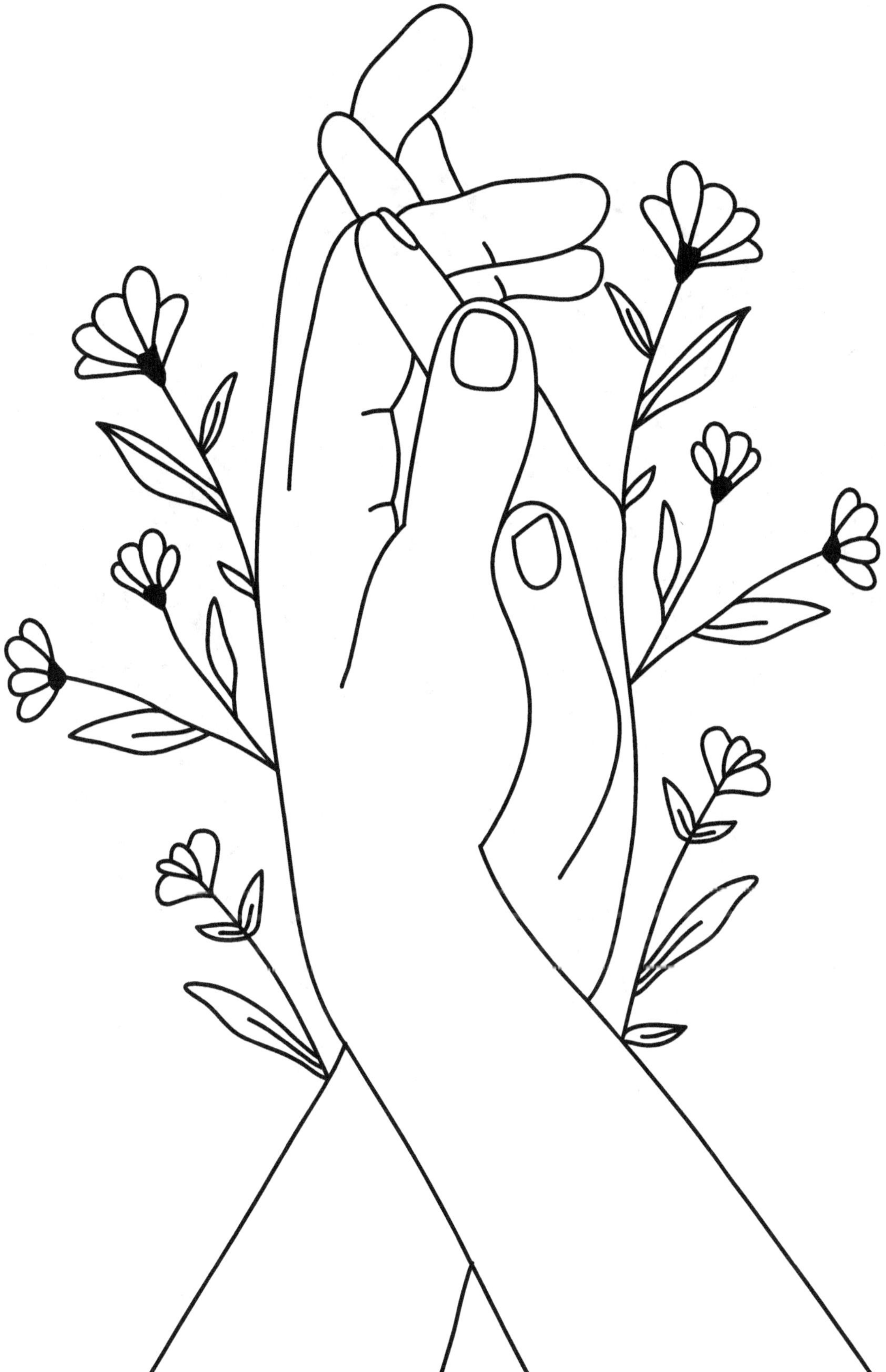

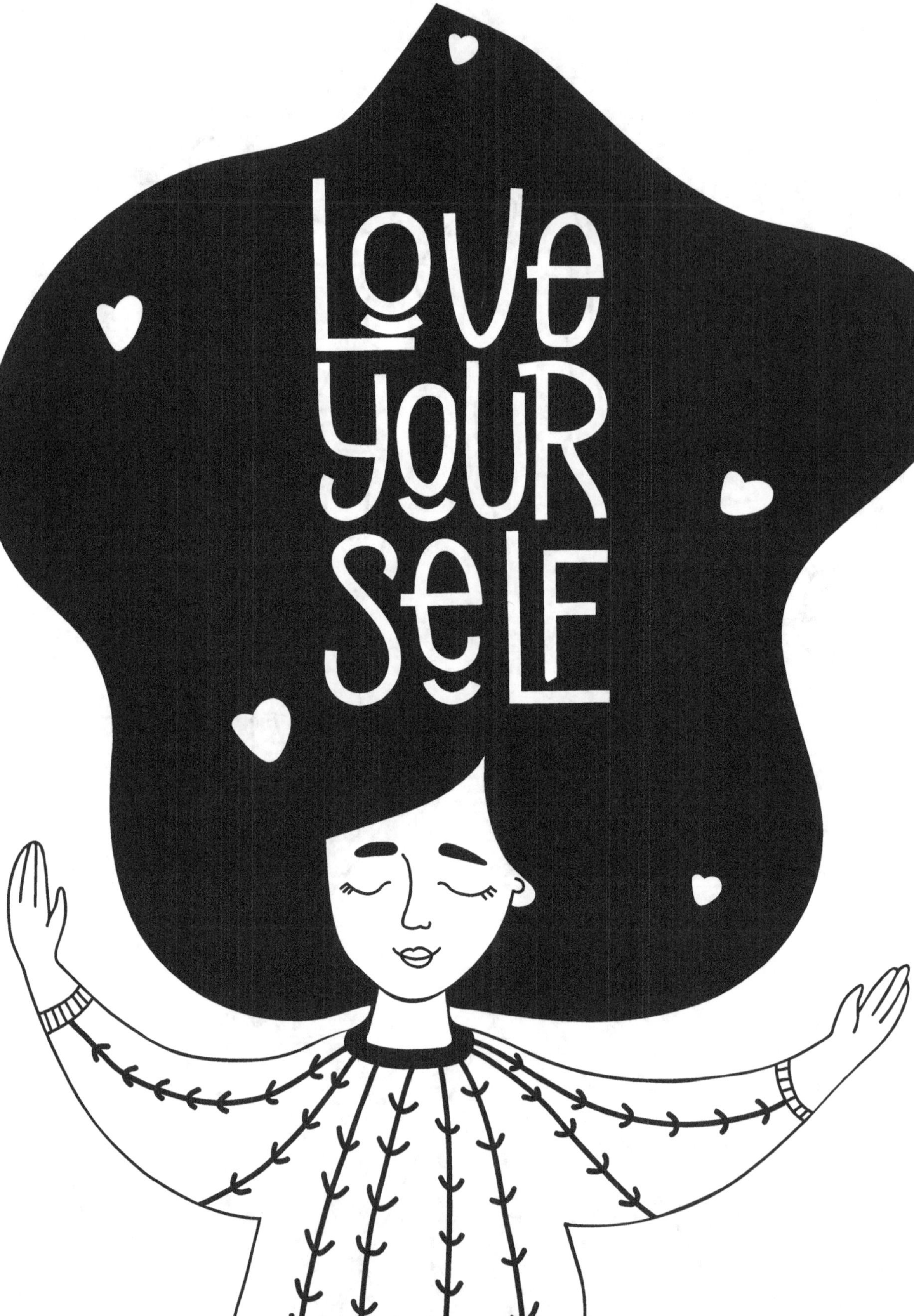
LOVE
YOUR
SELF

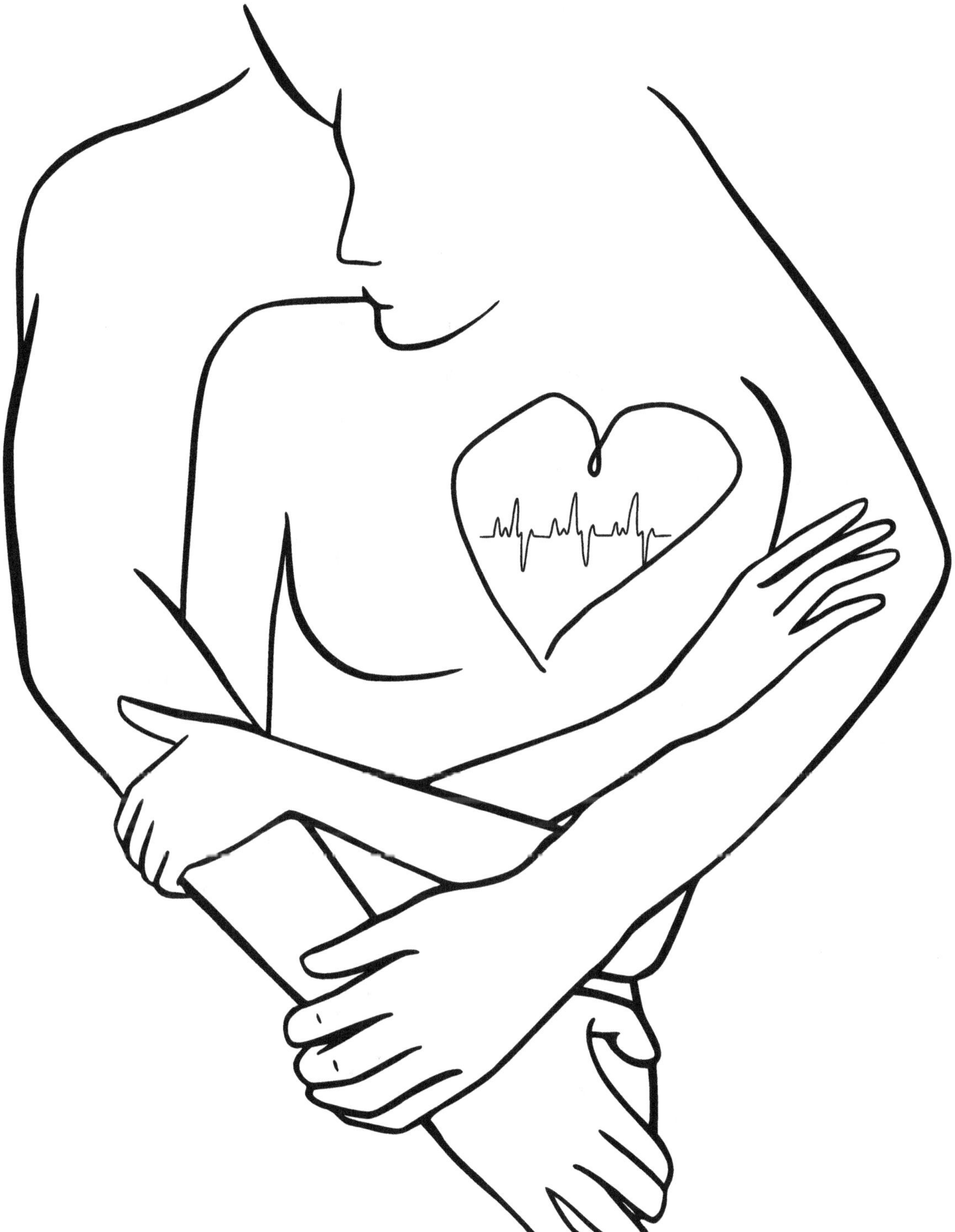

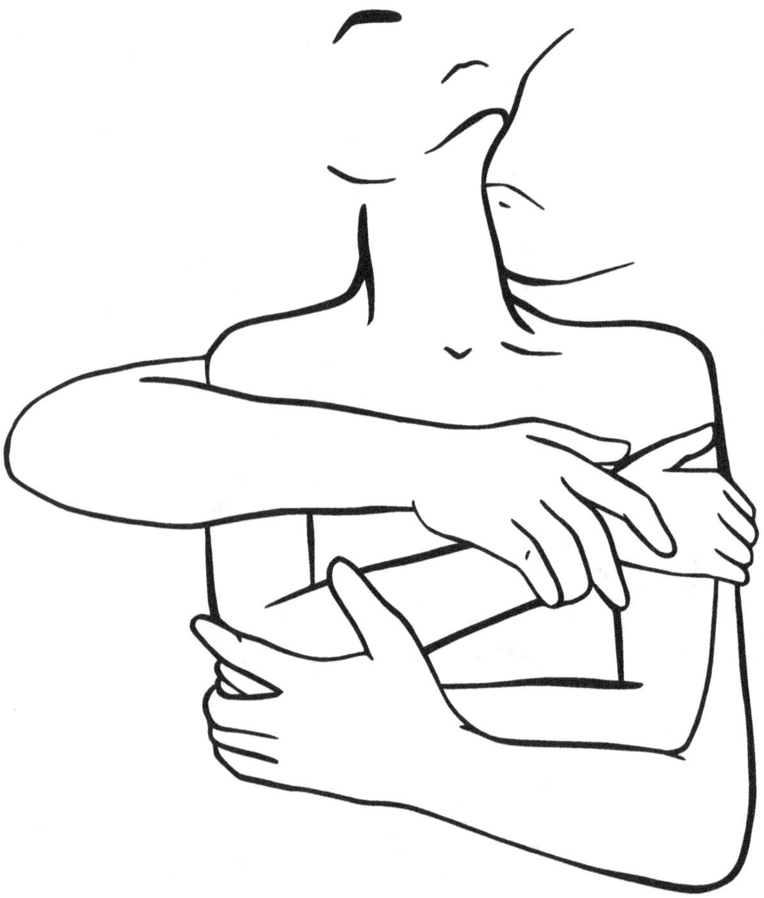

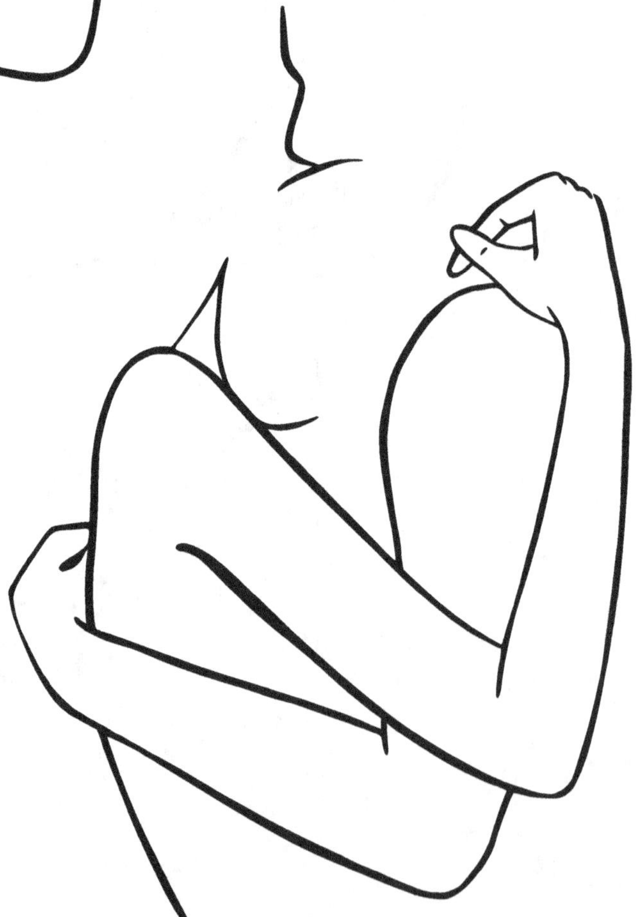

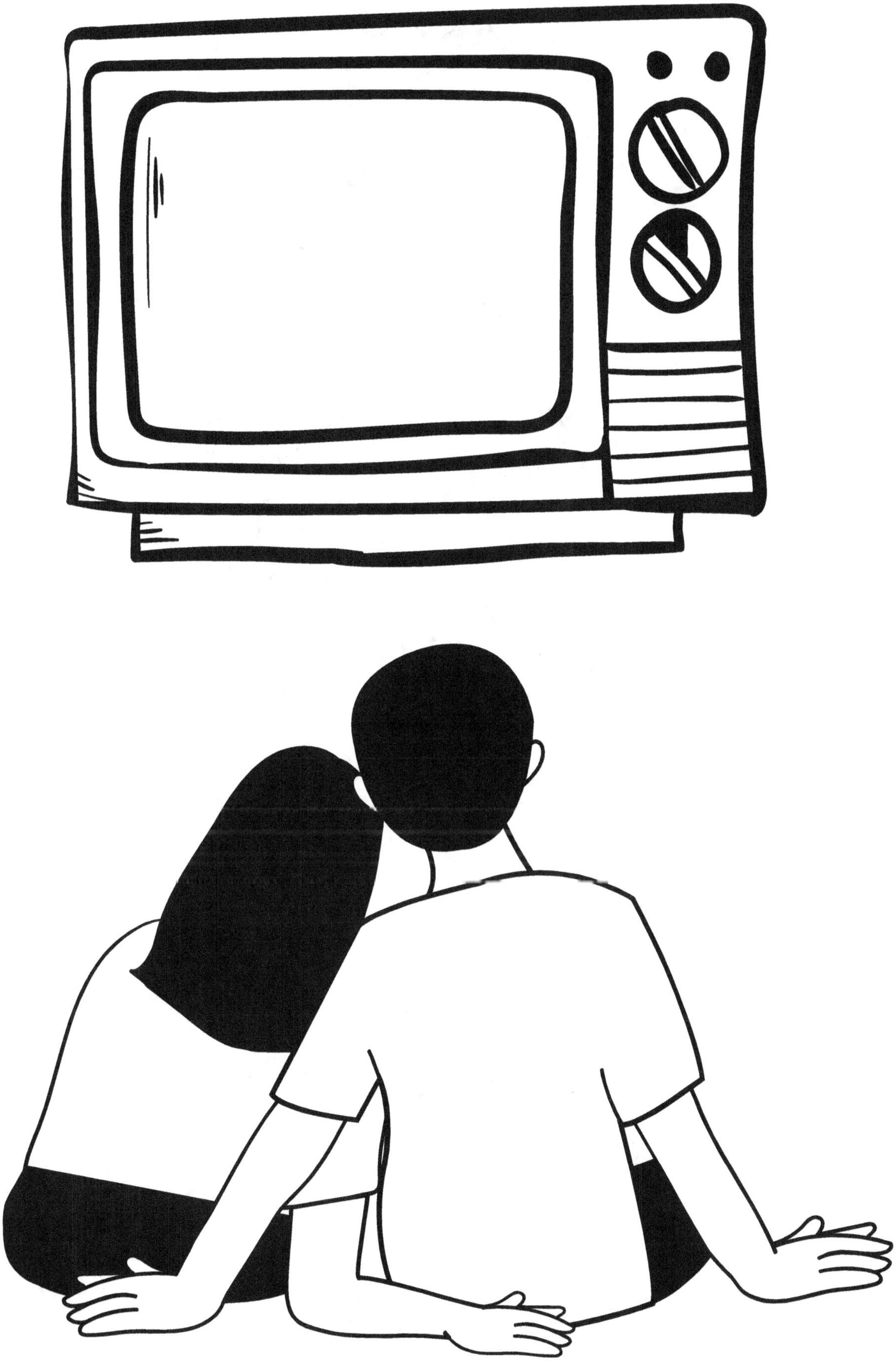

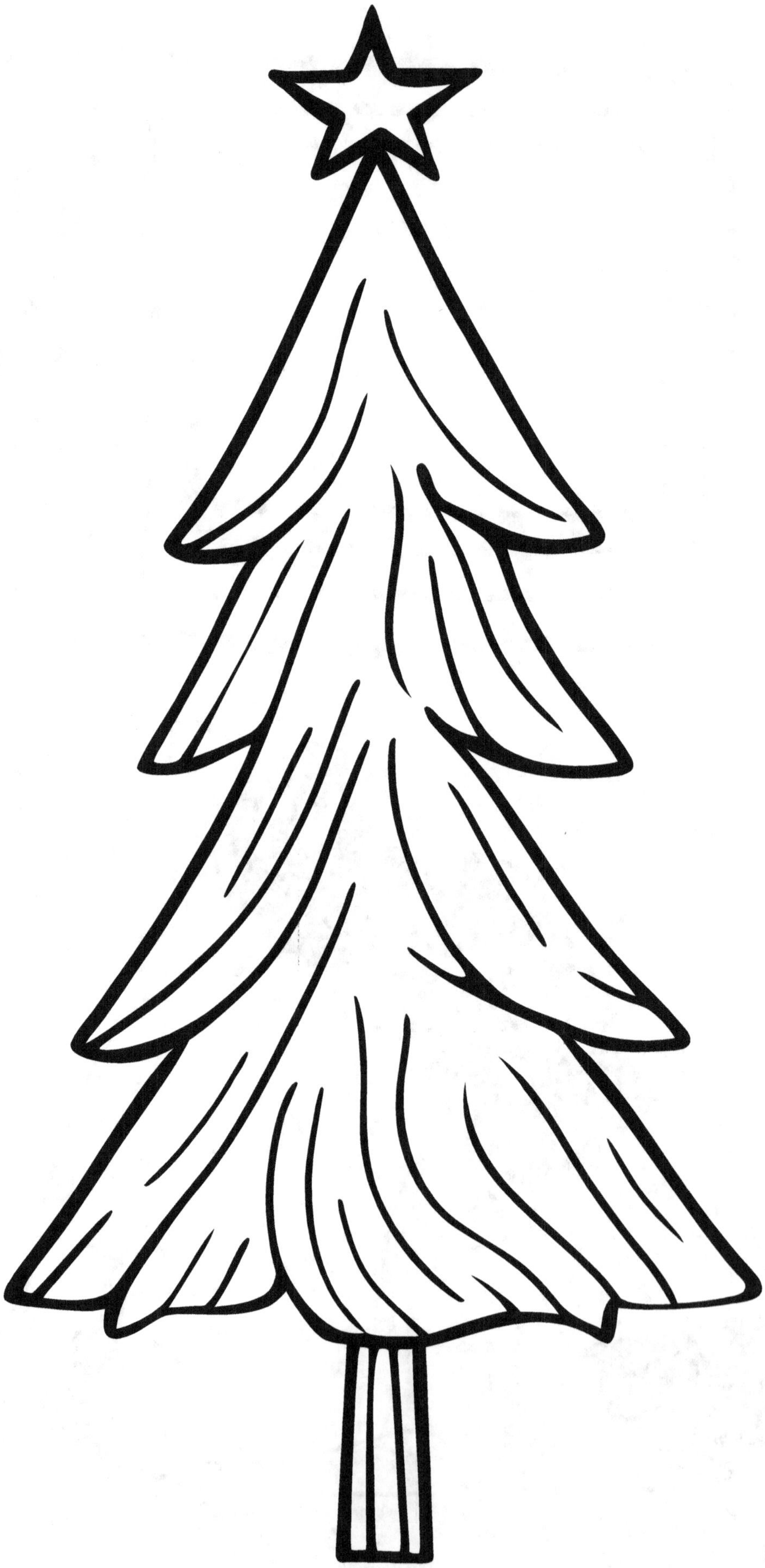

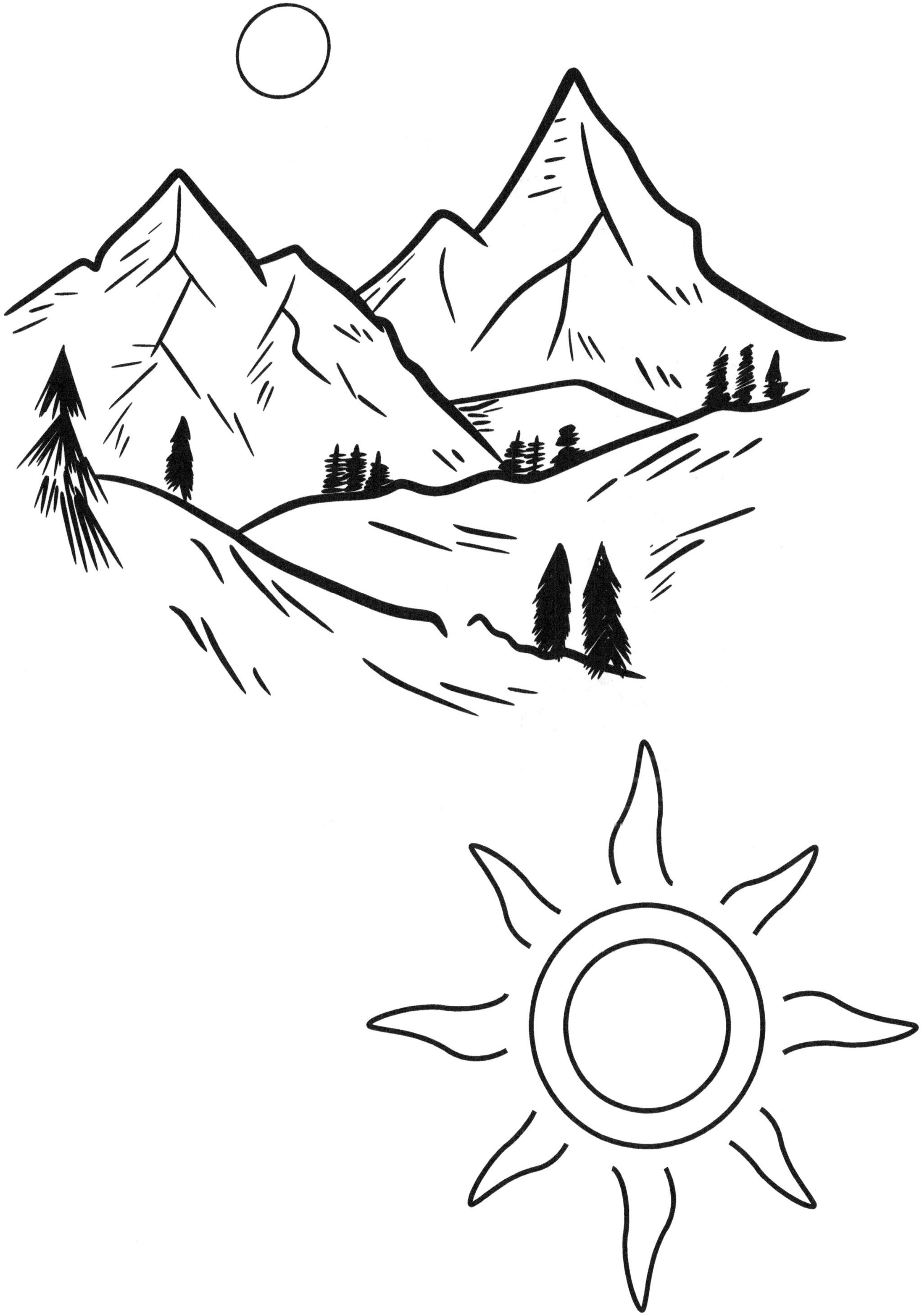

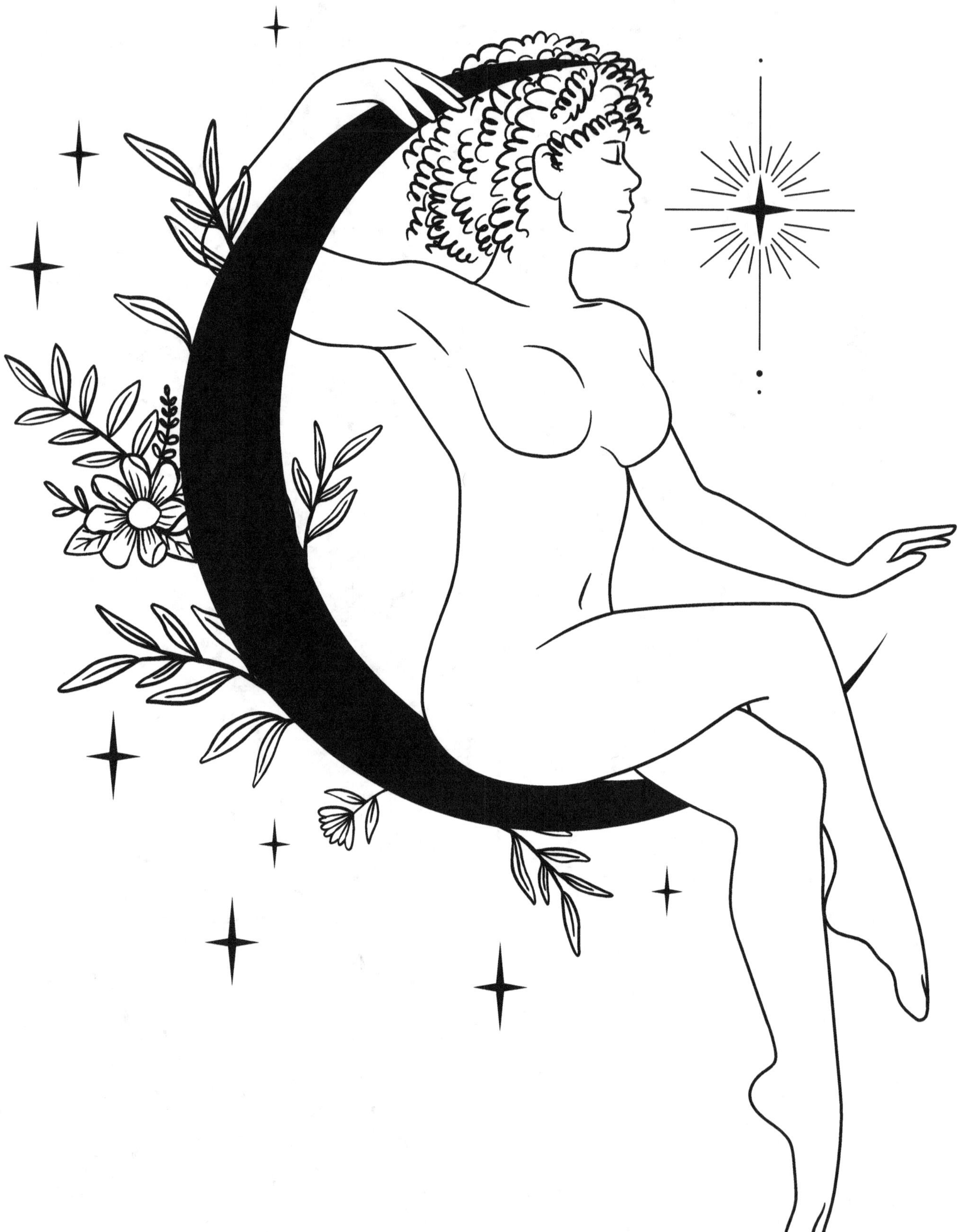

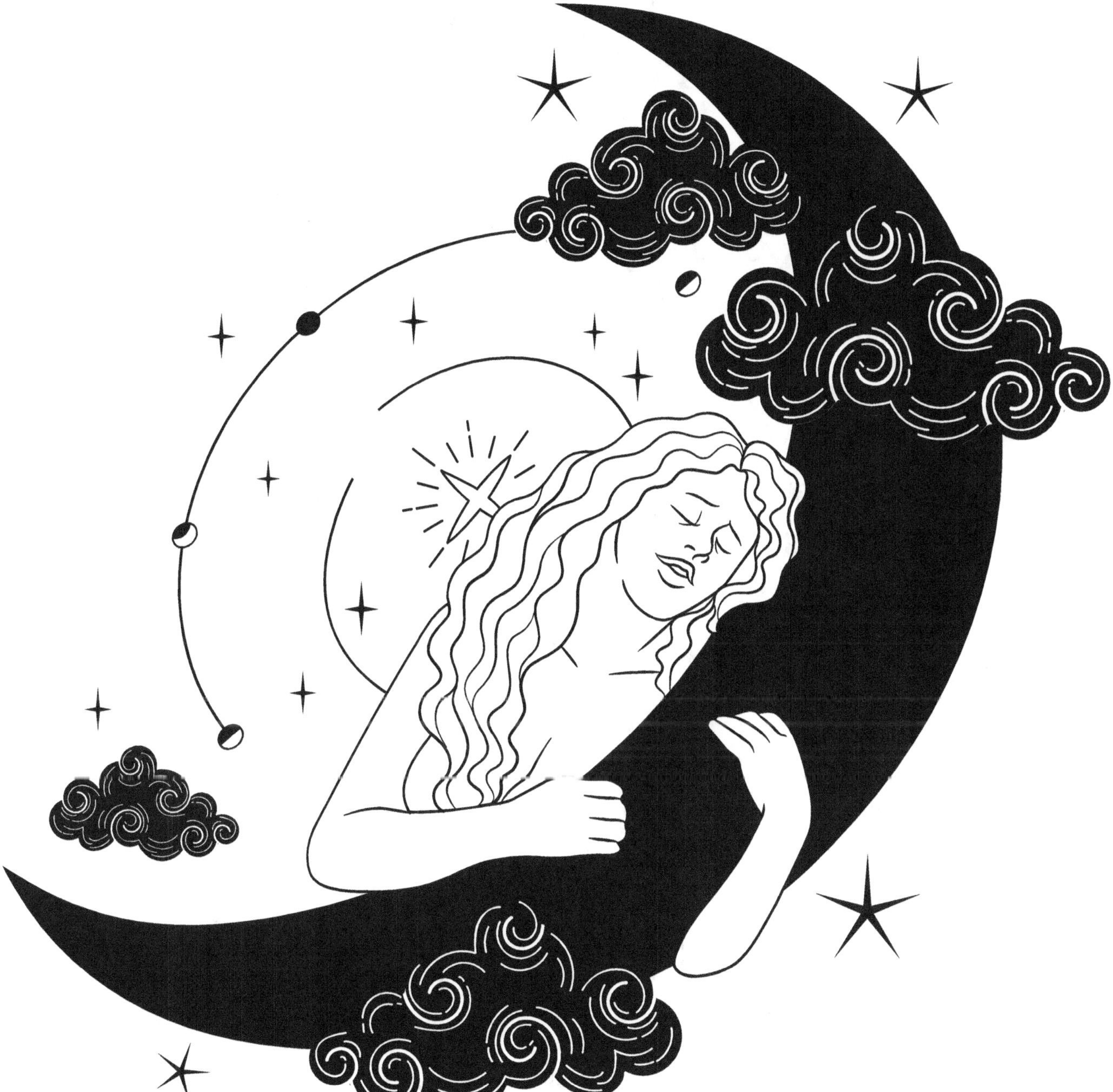

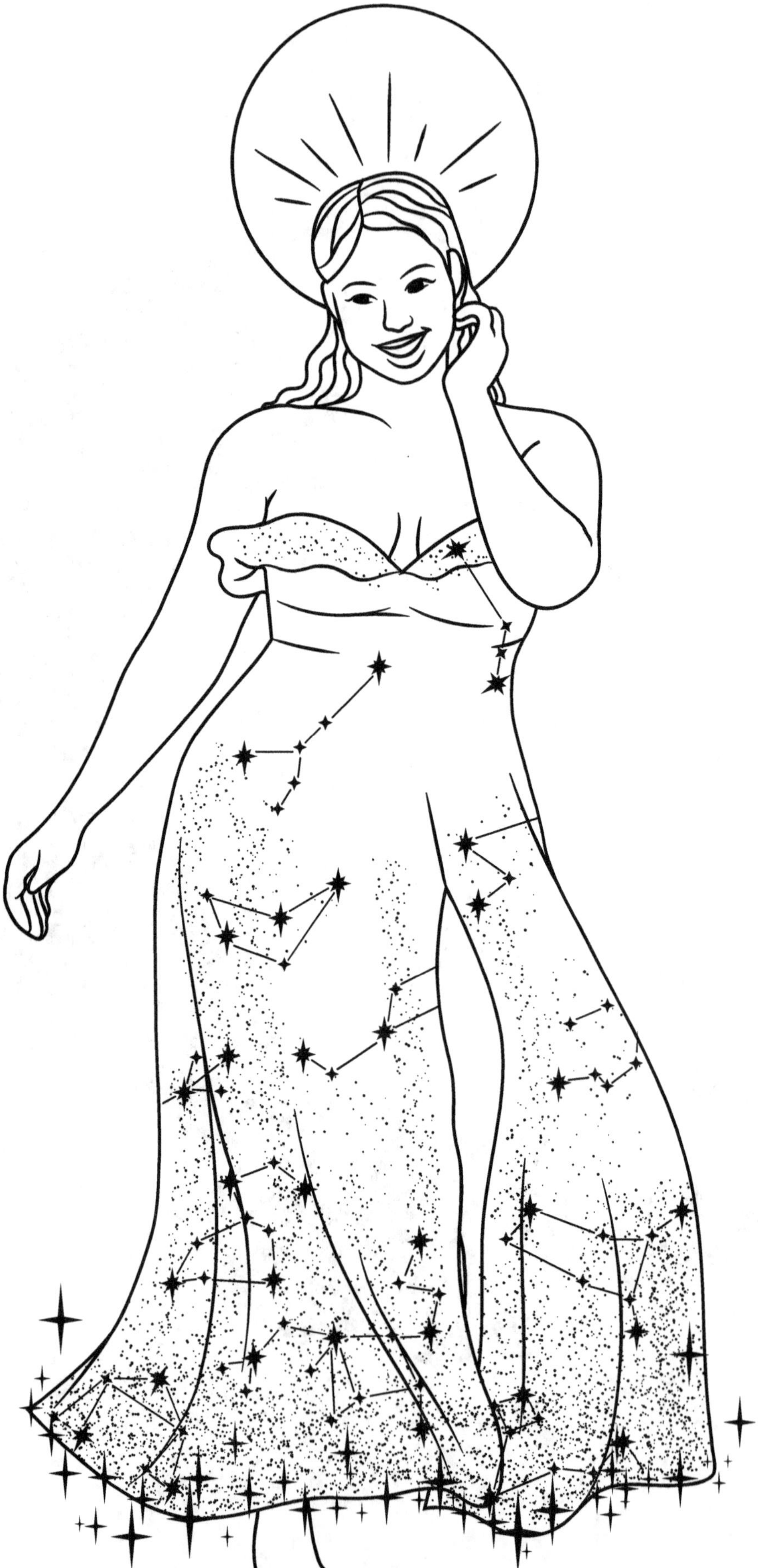

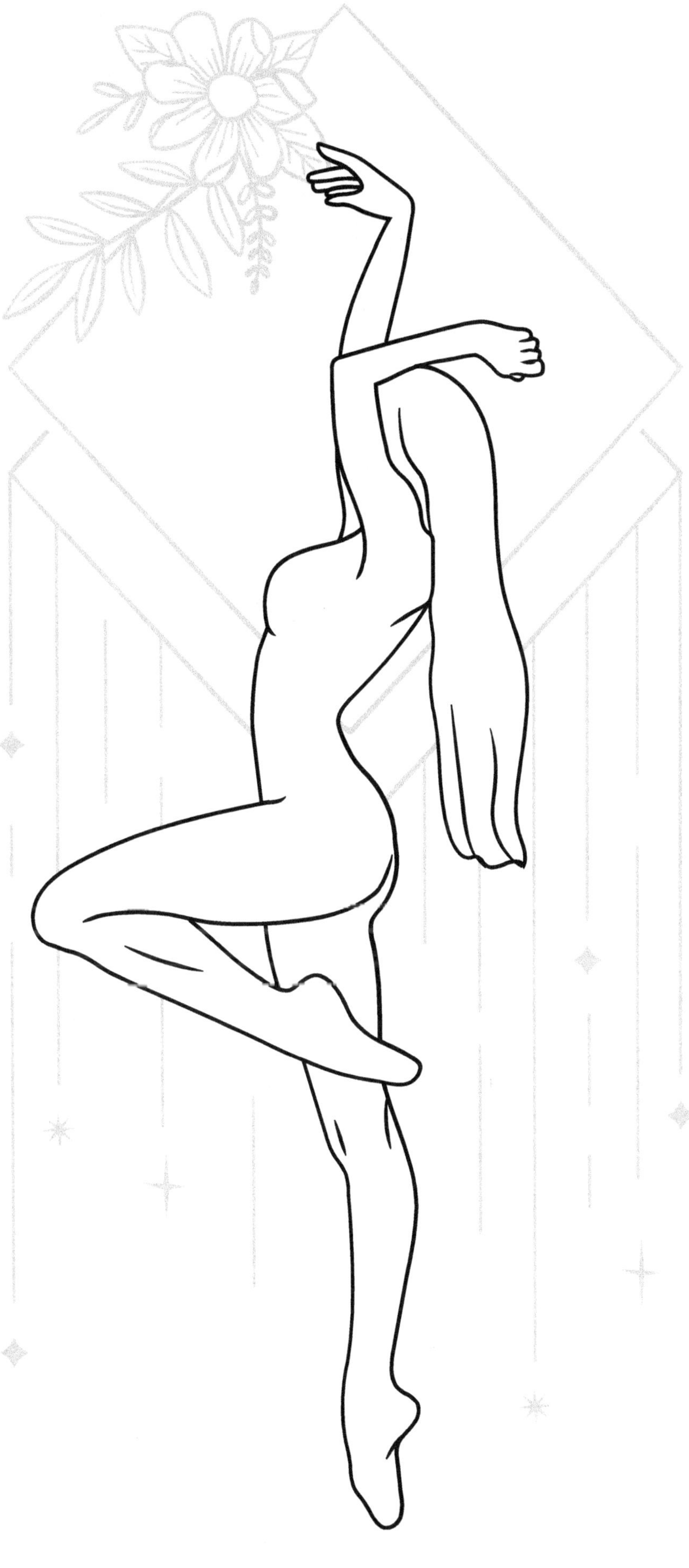

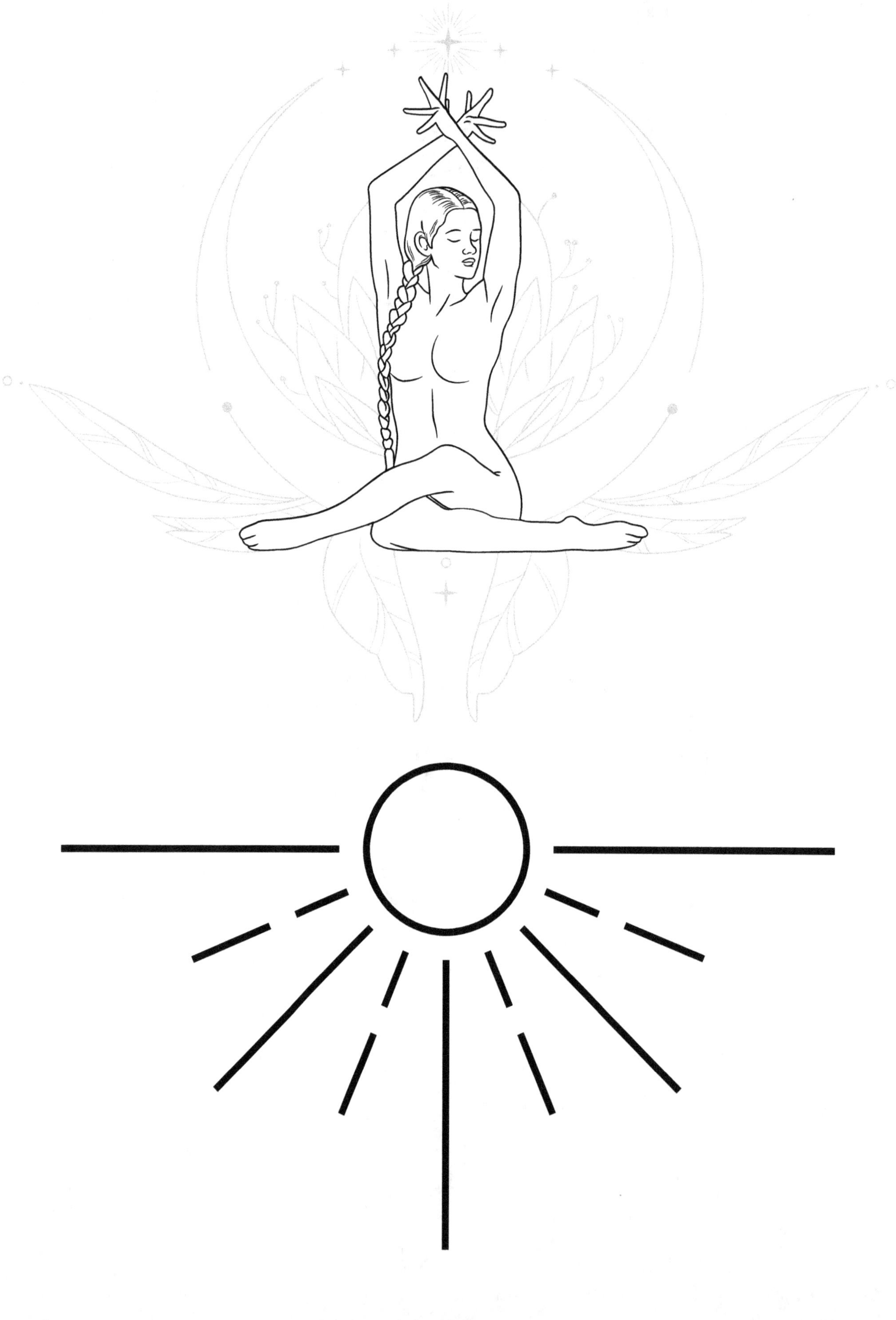

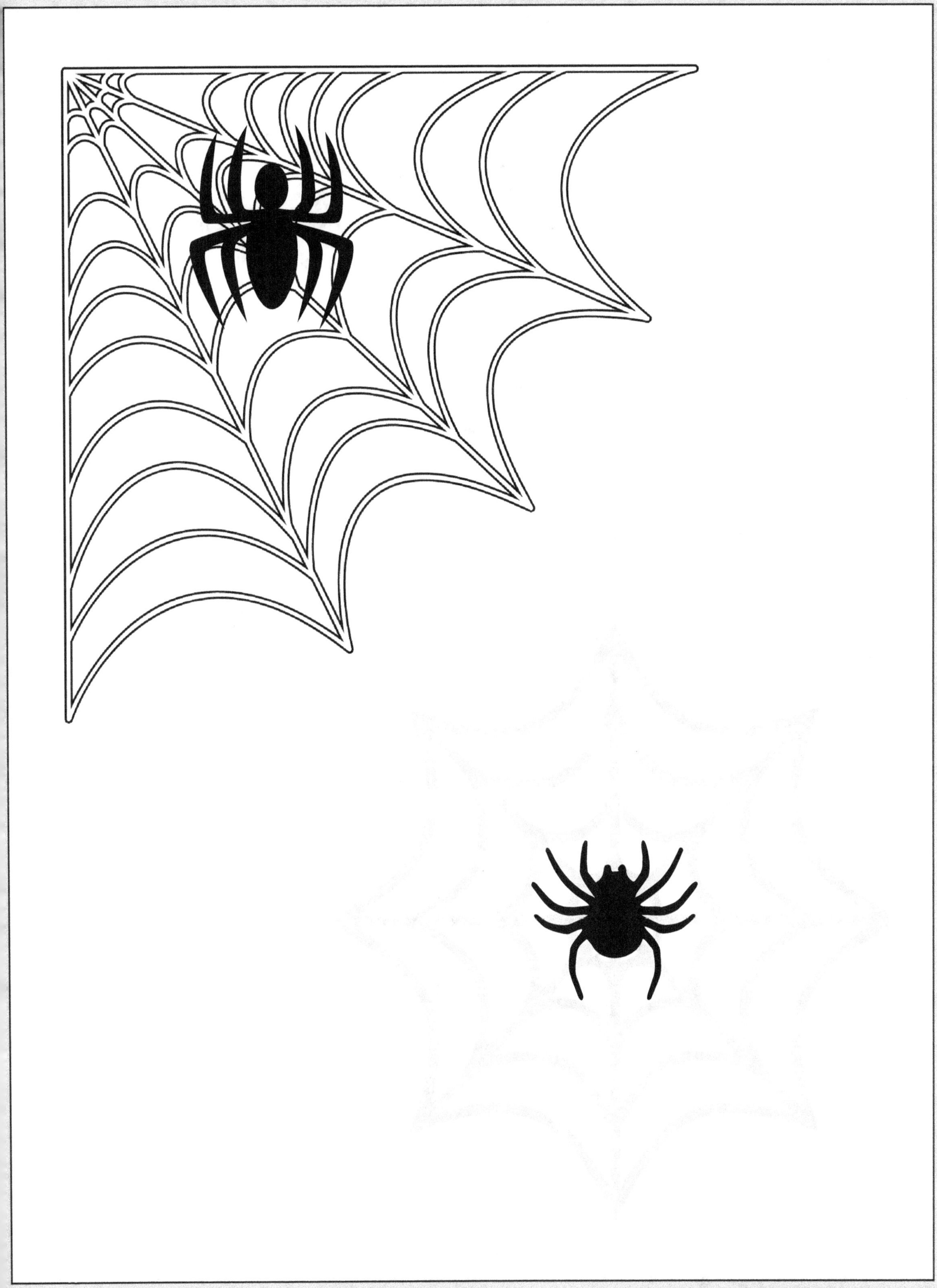

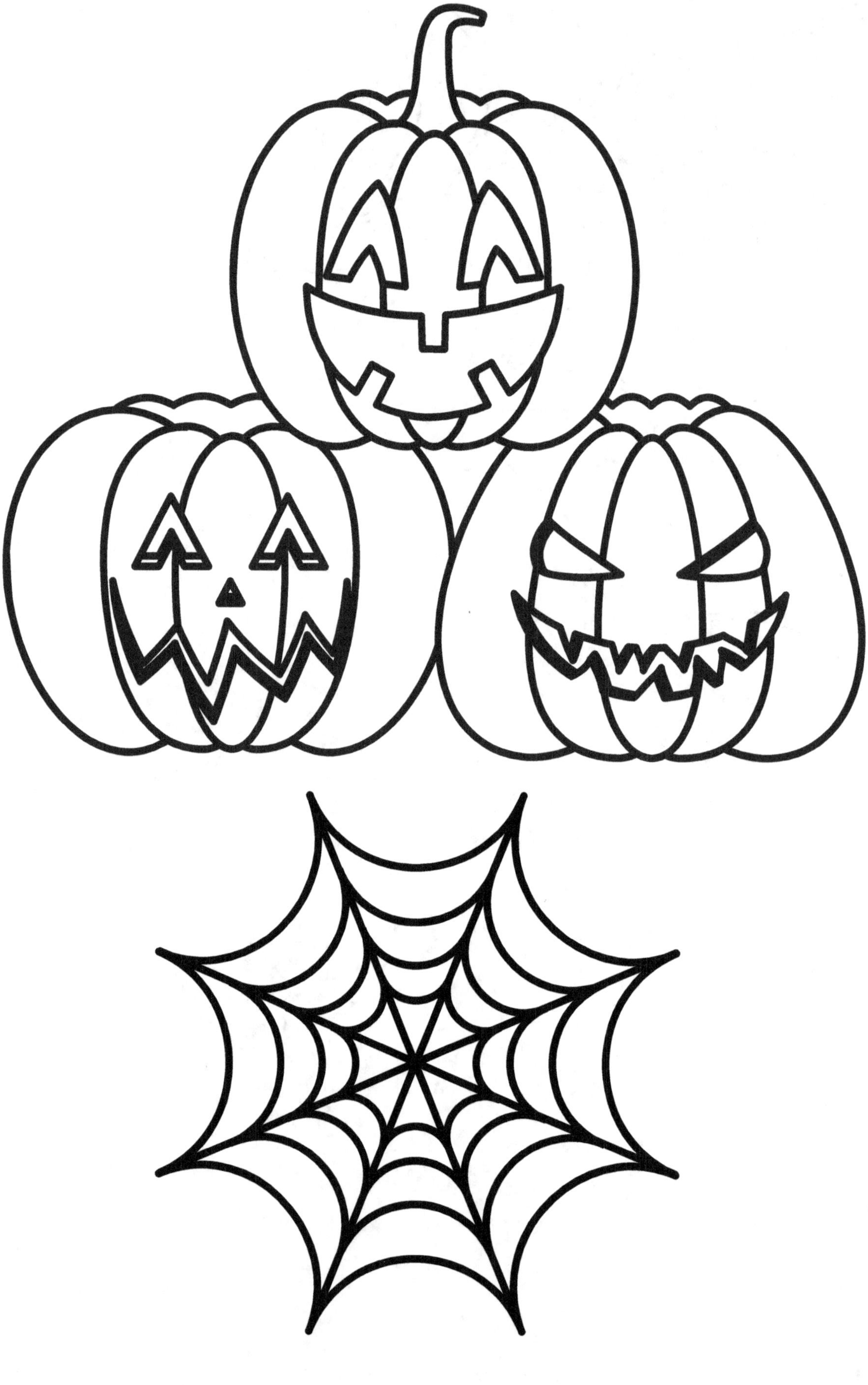

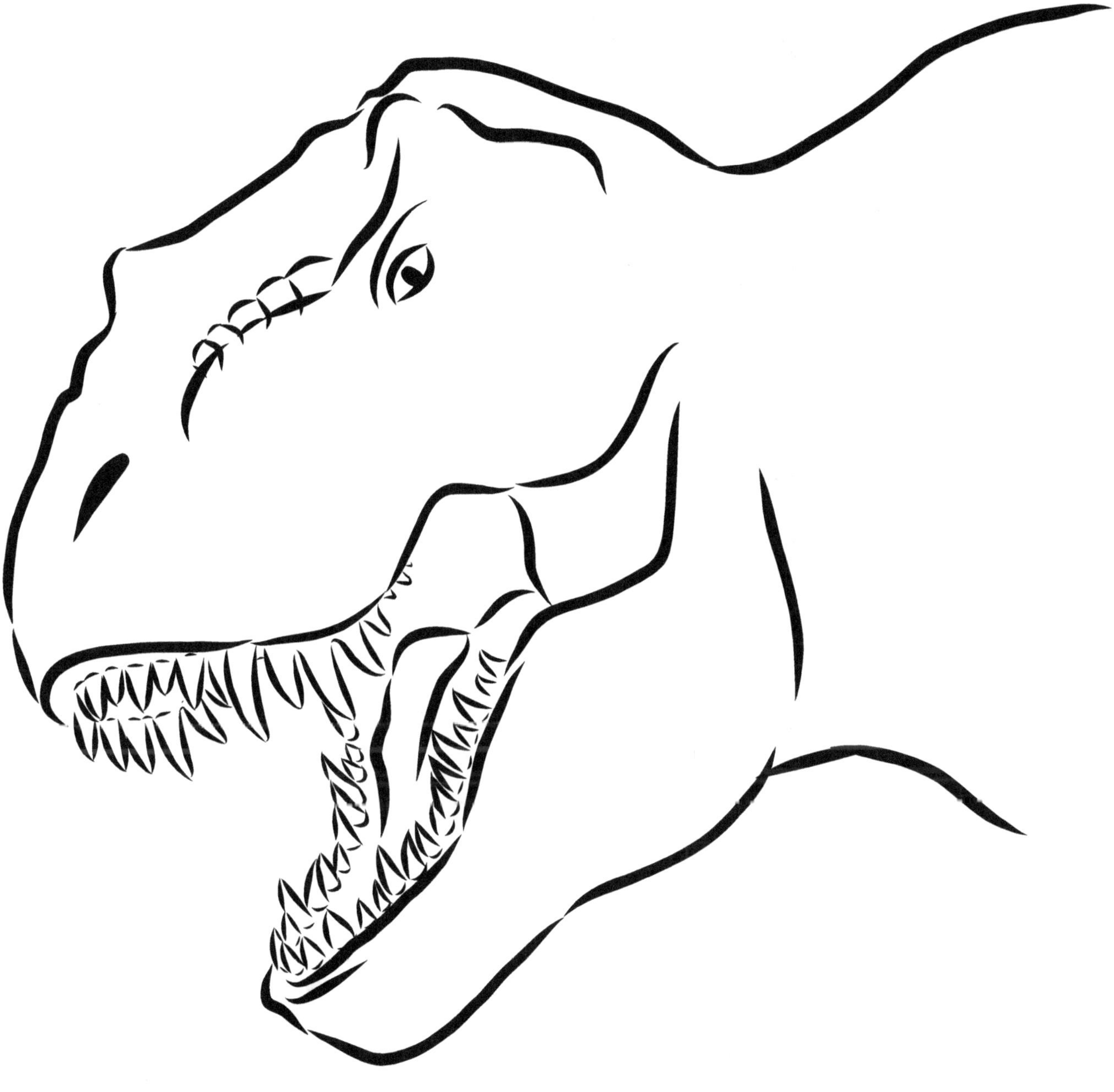

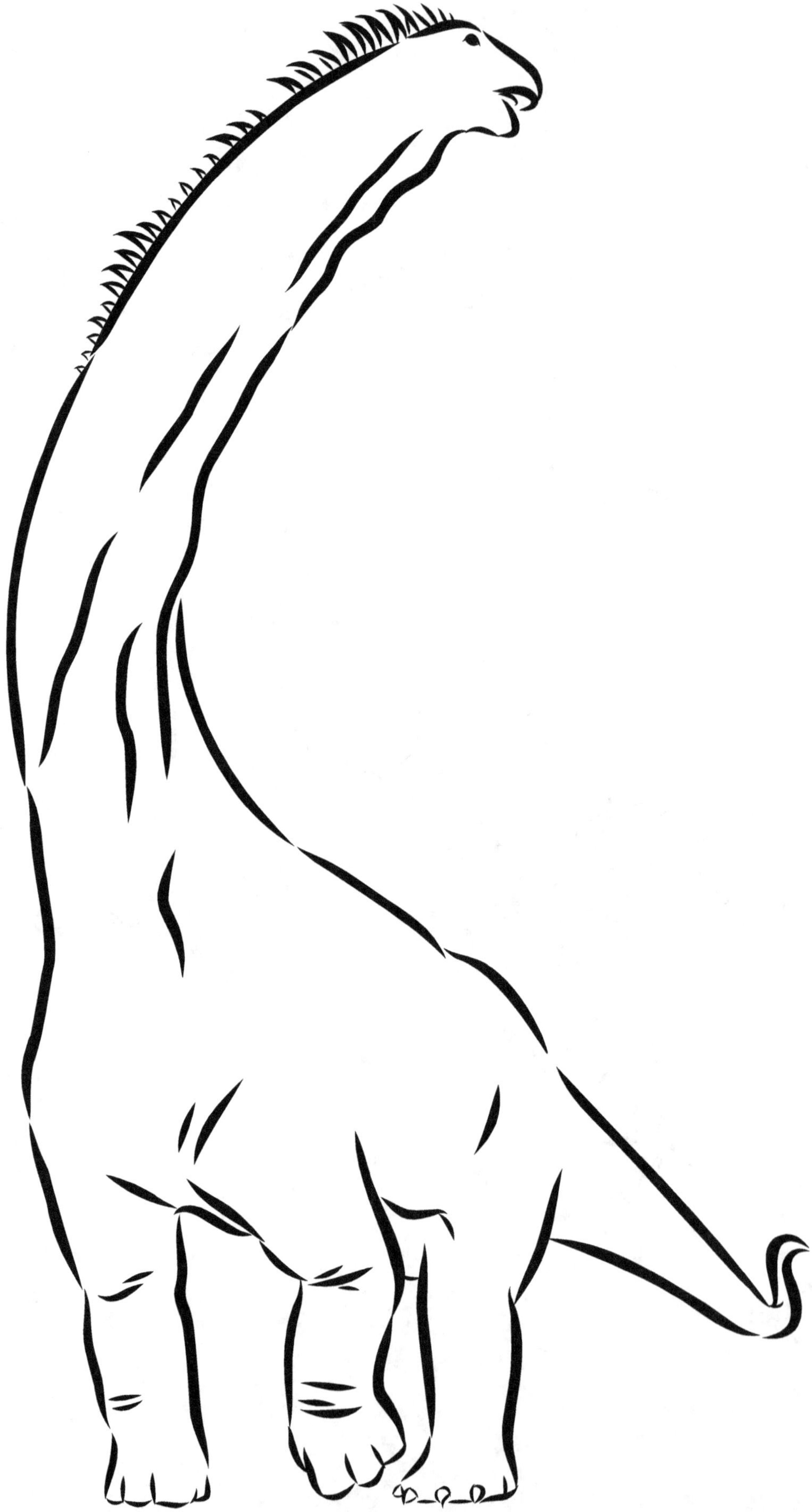

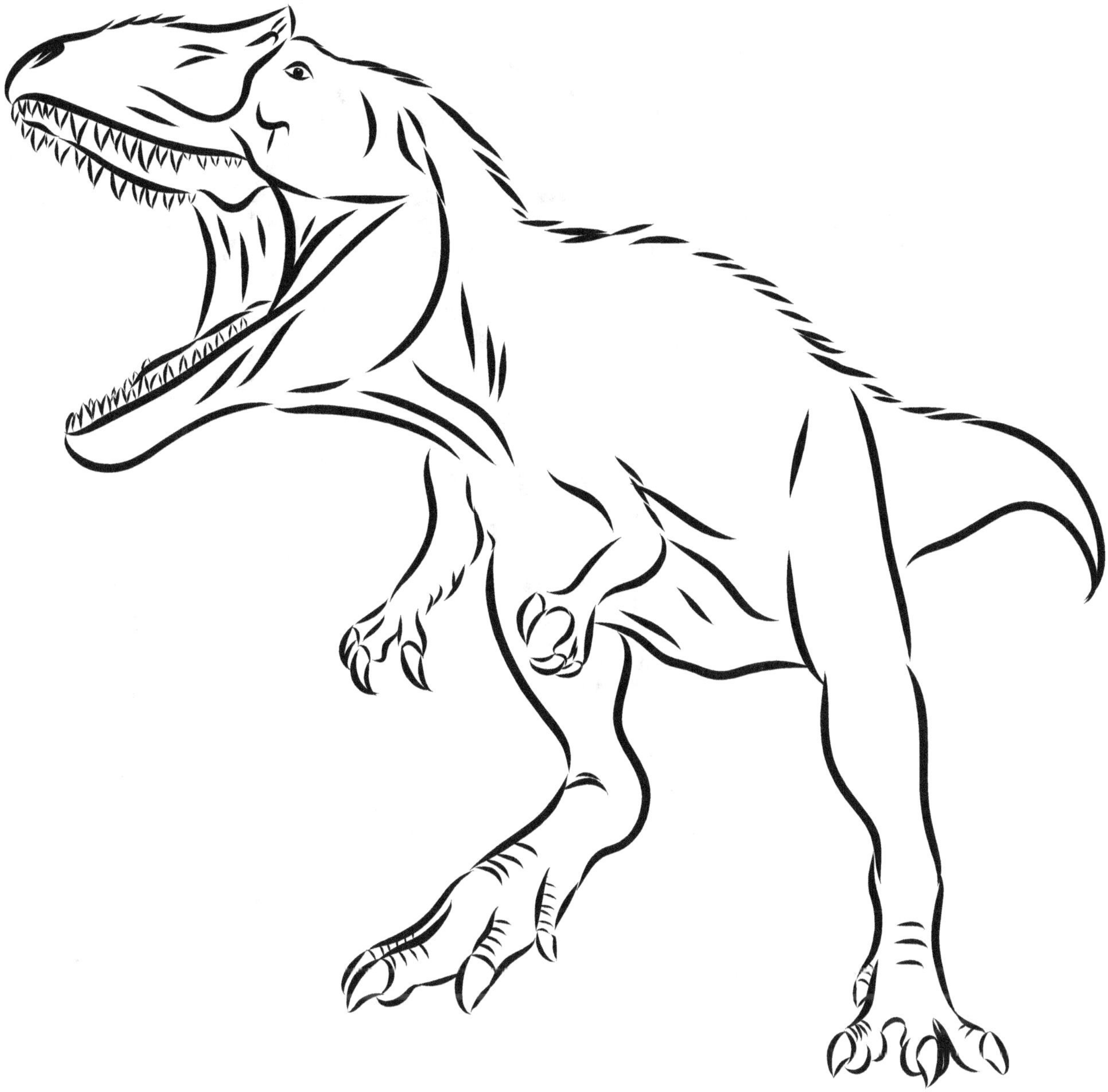

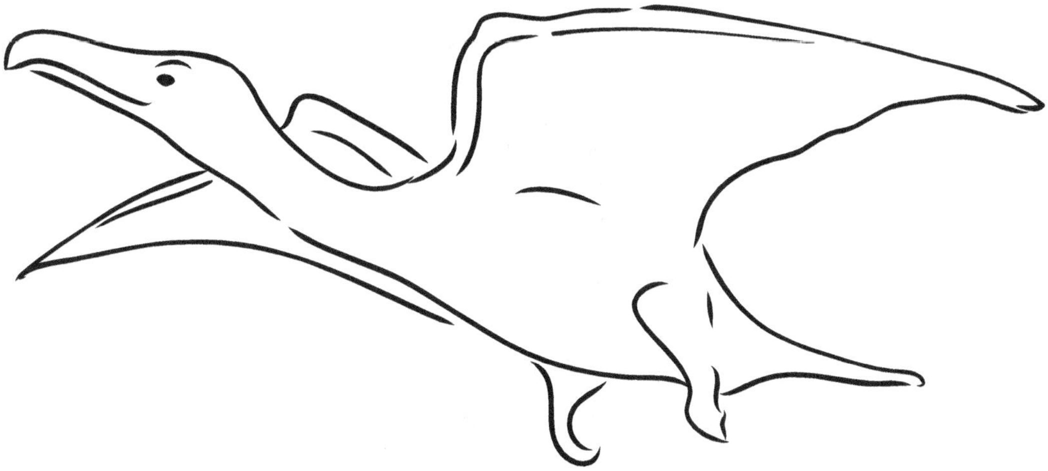

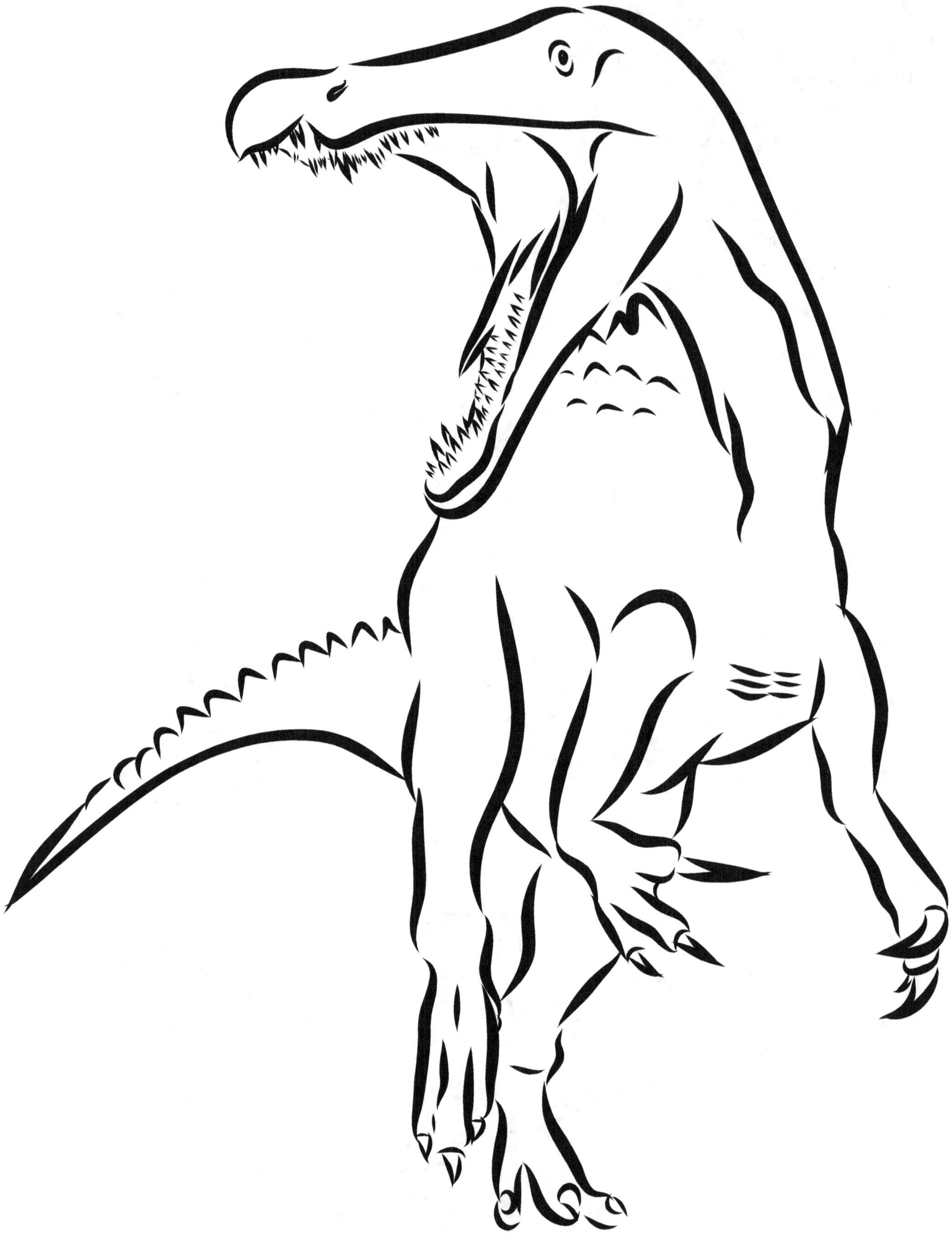

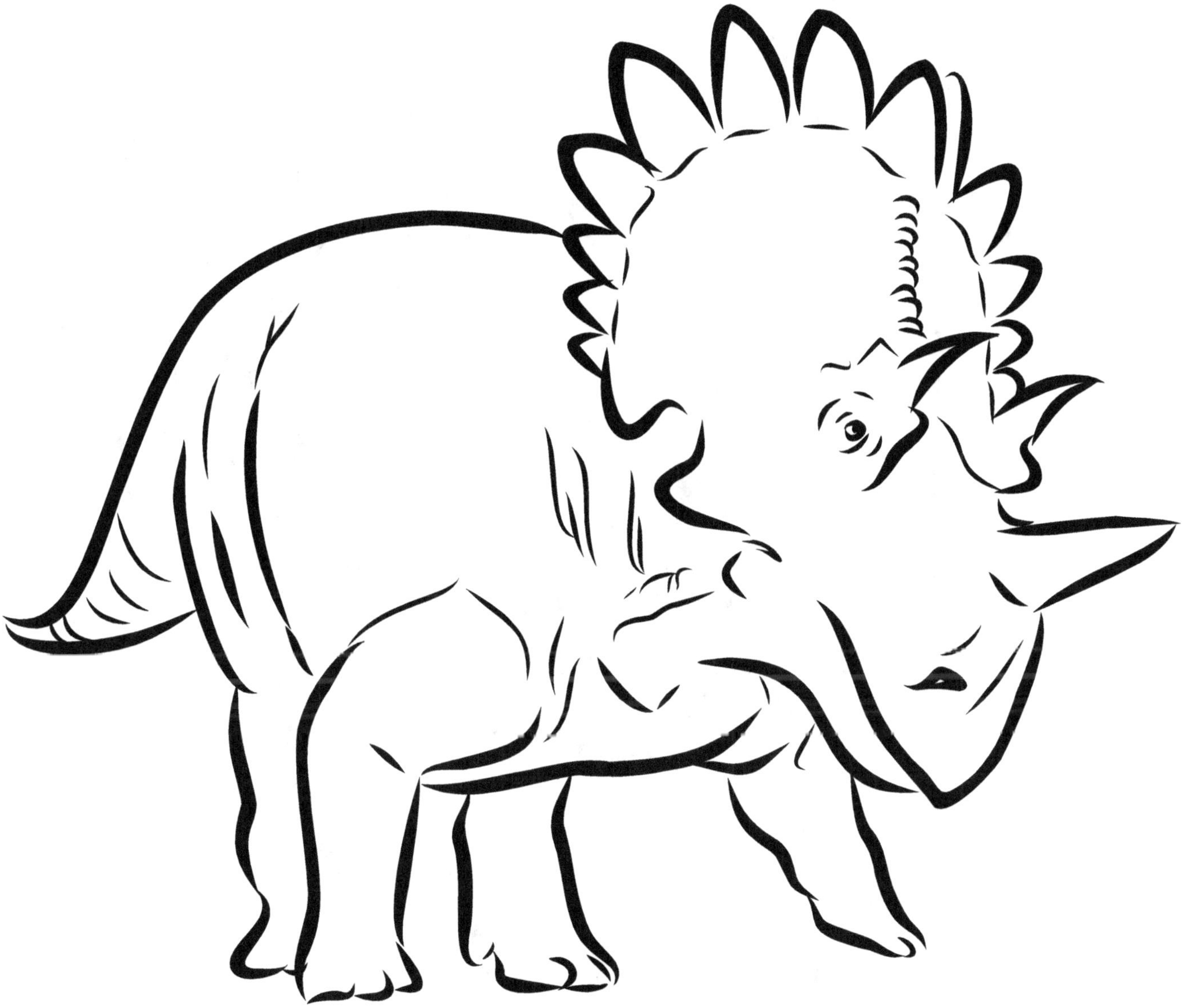

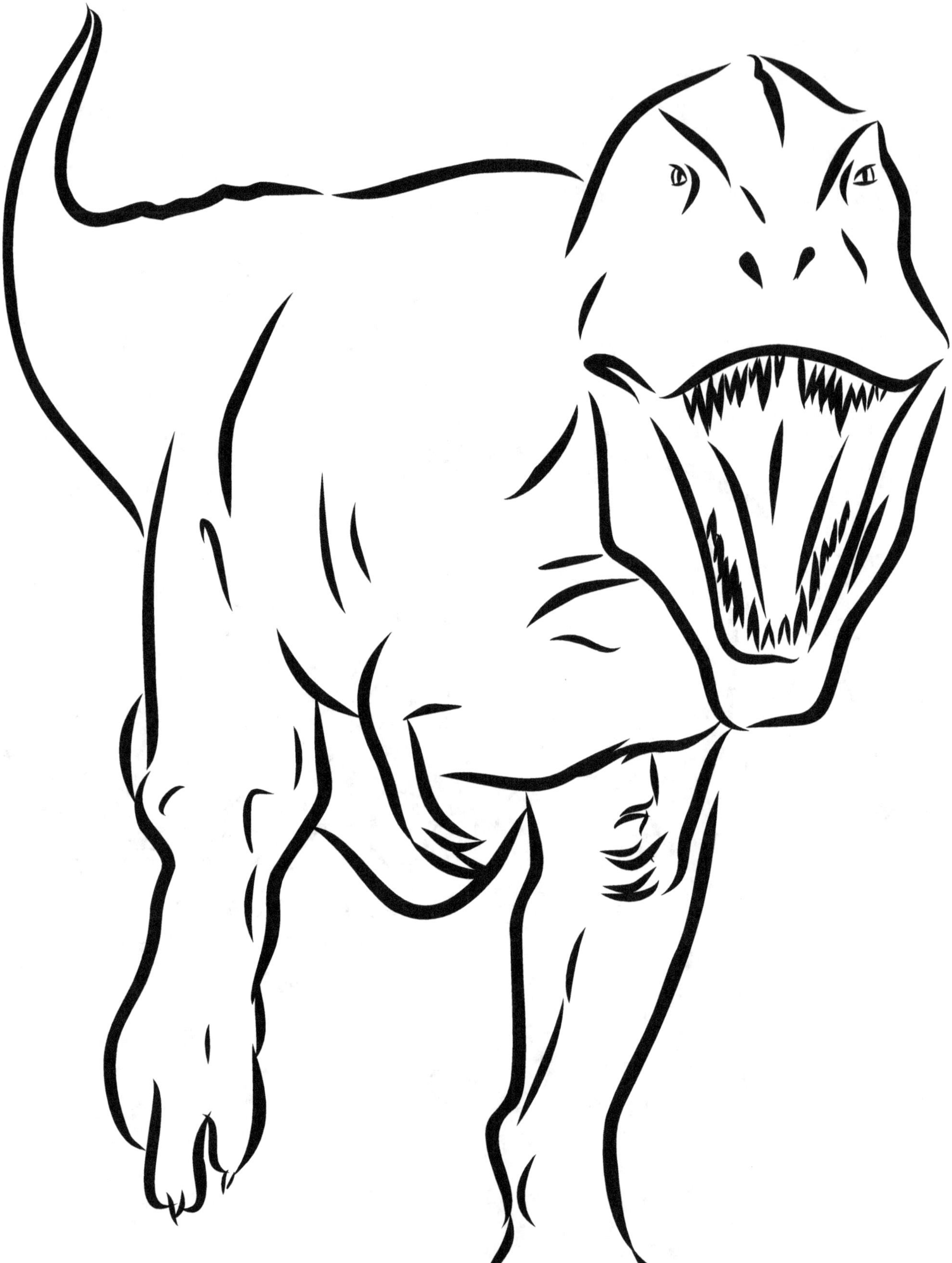

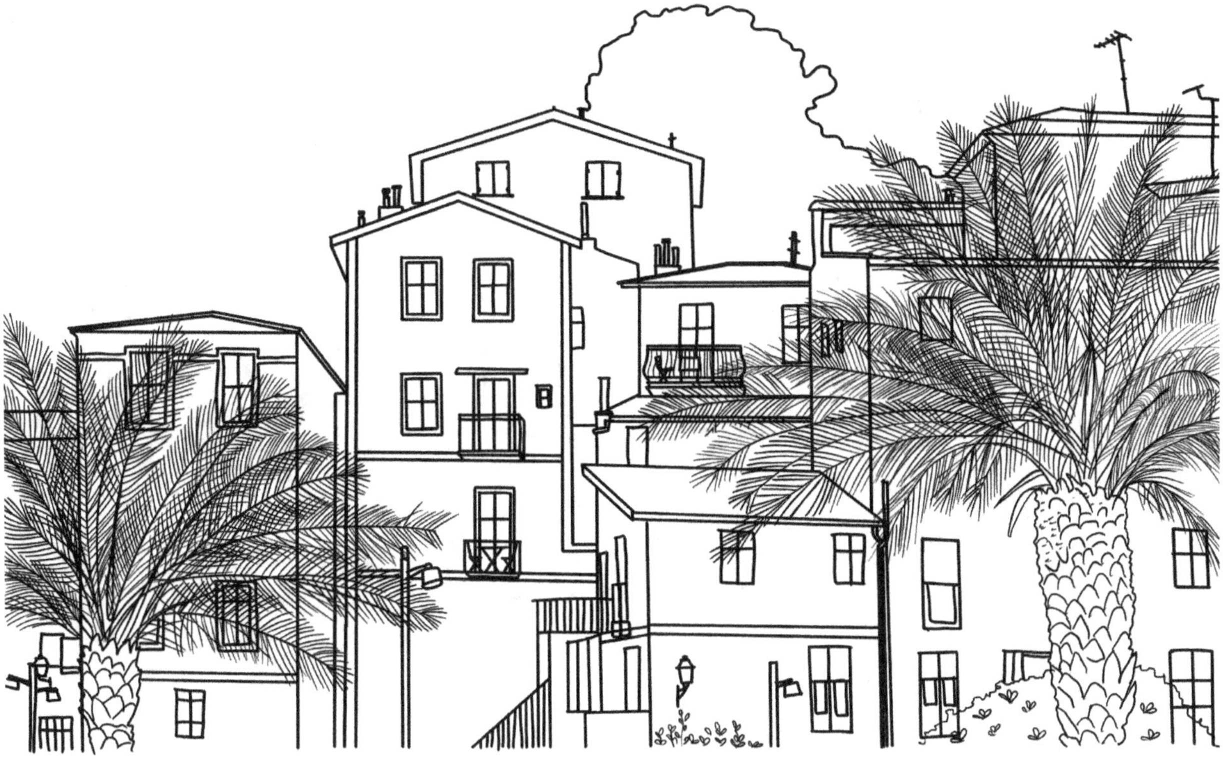

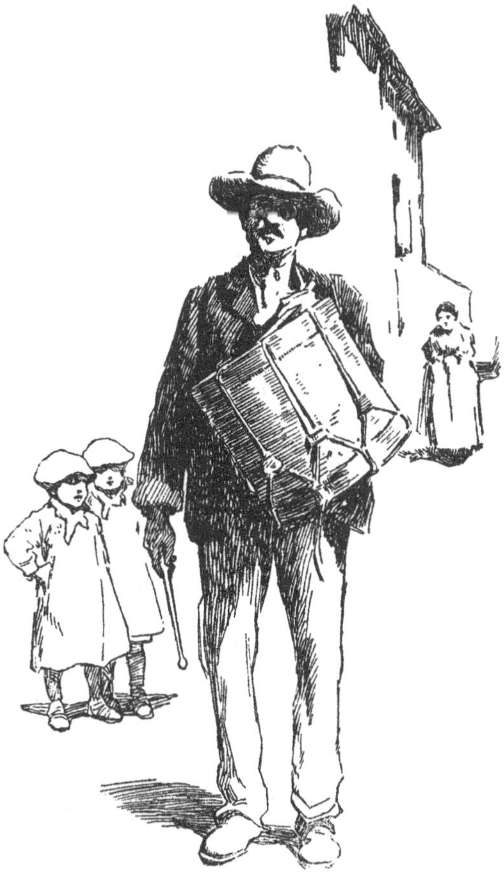

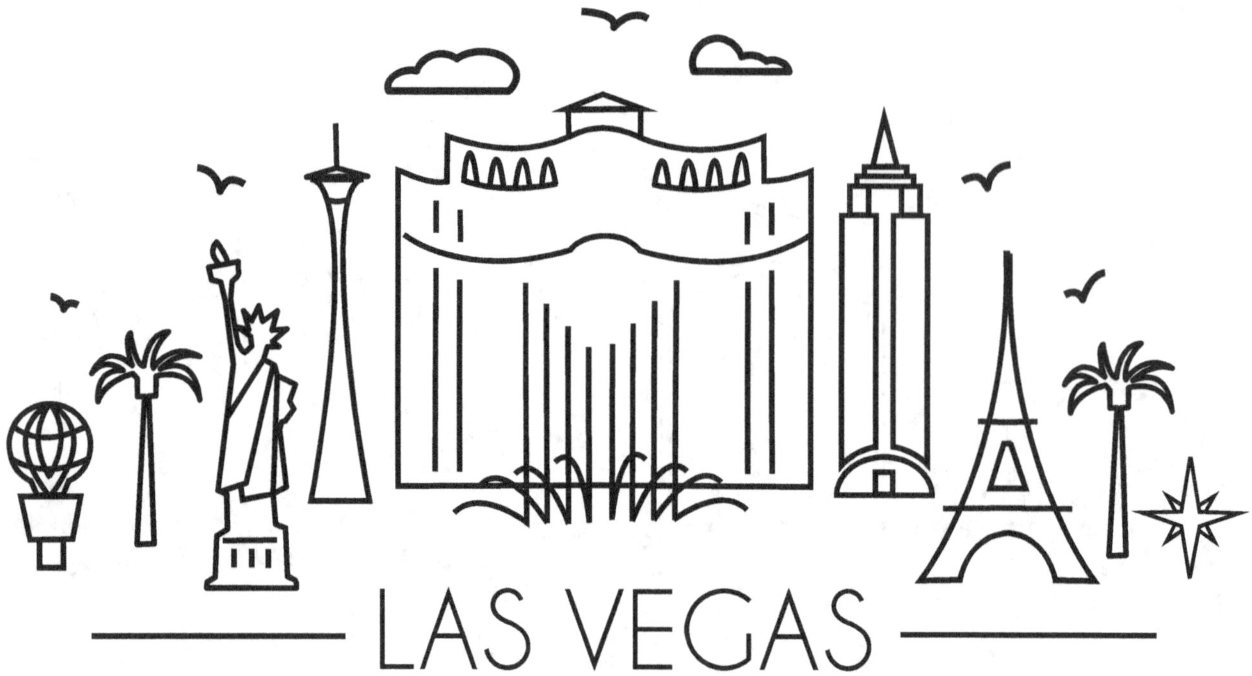
LAS VEGAS

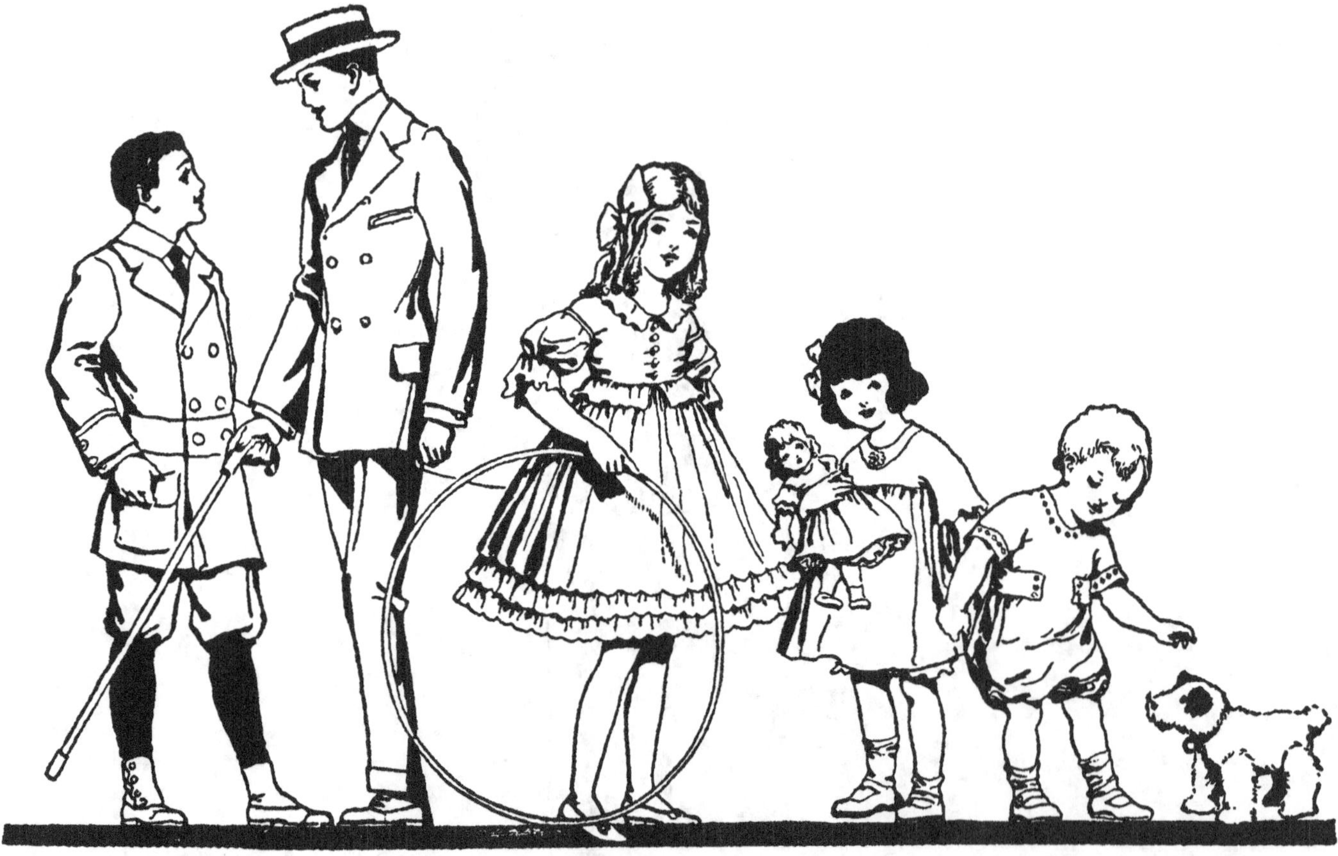

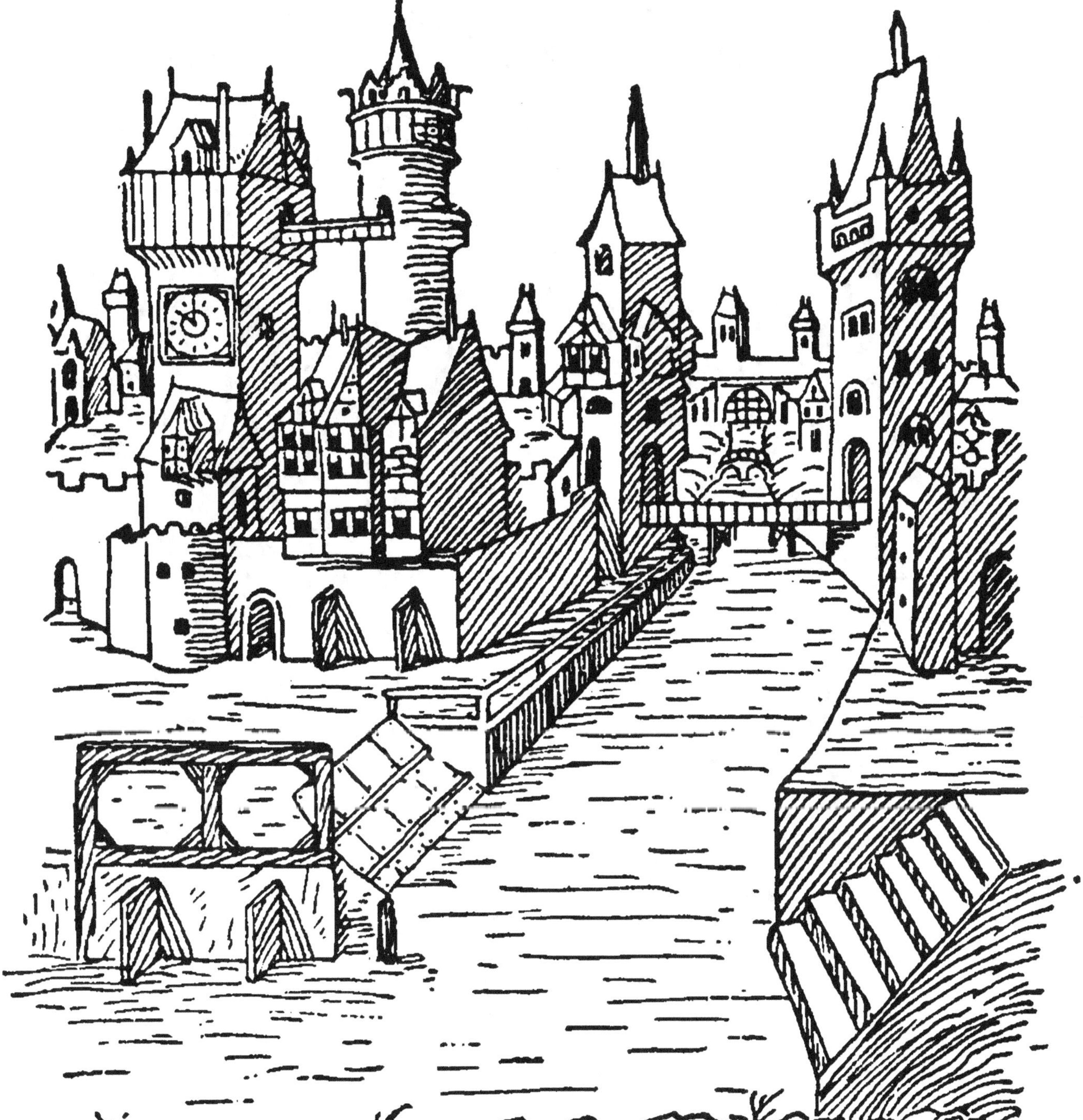

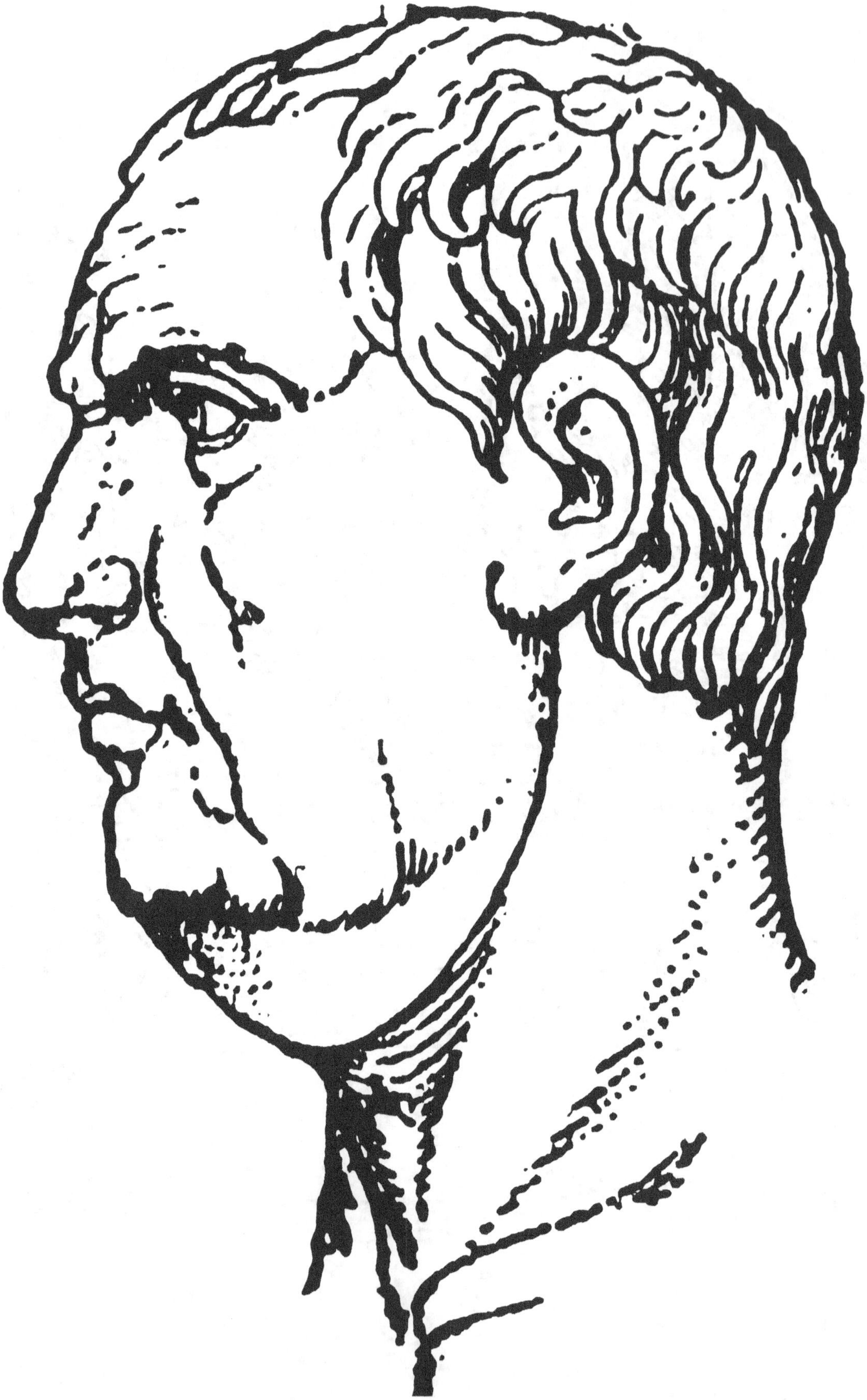

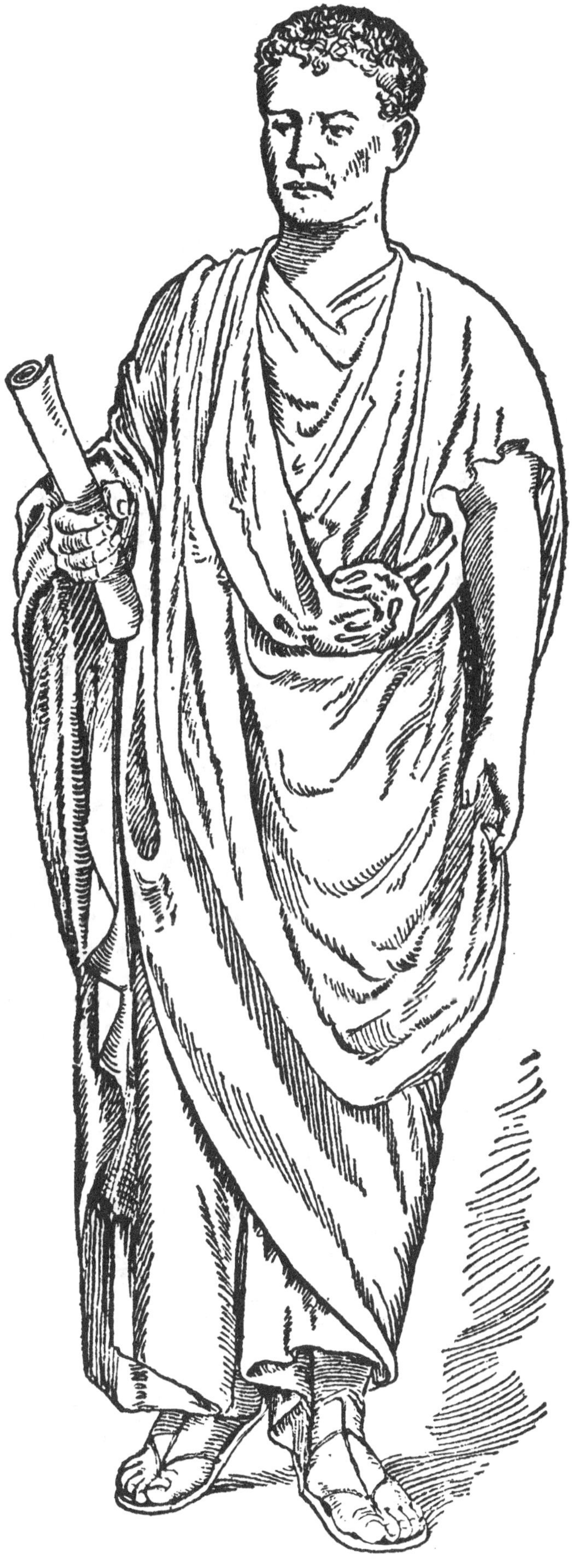

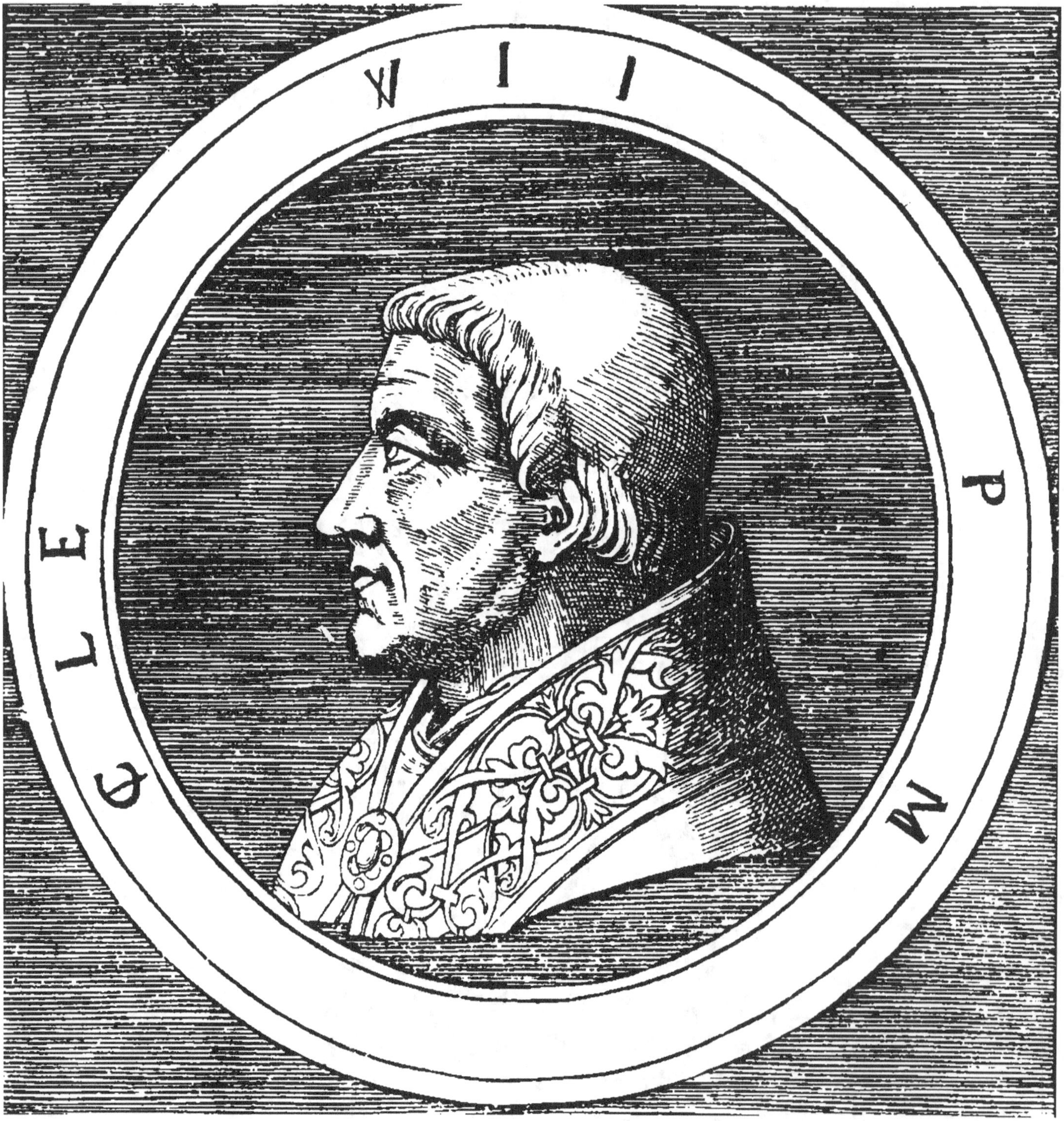

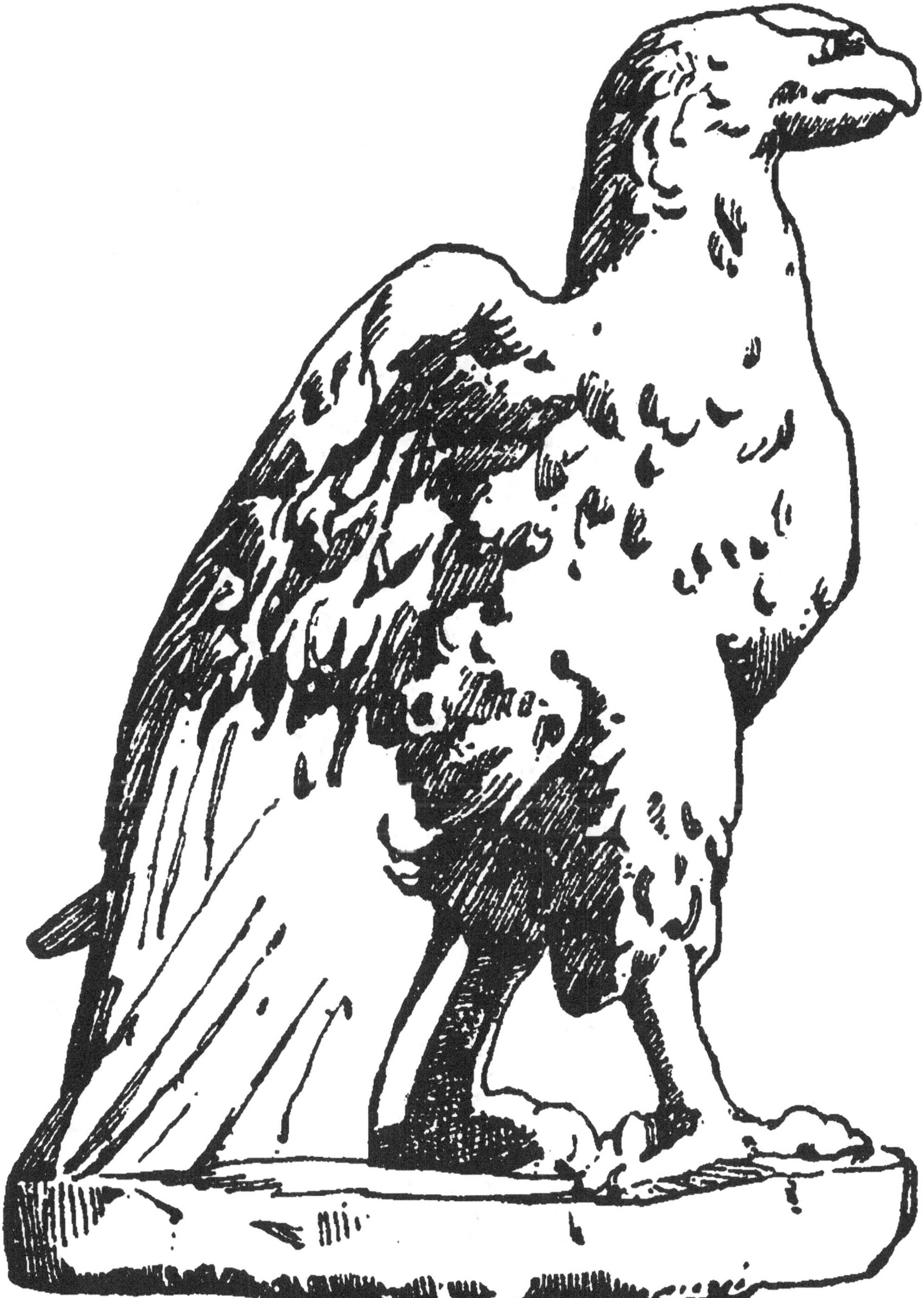

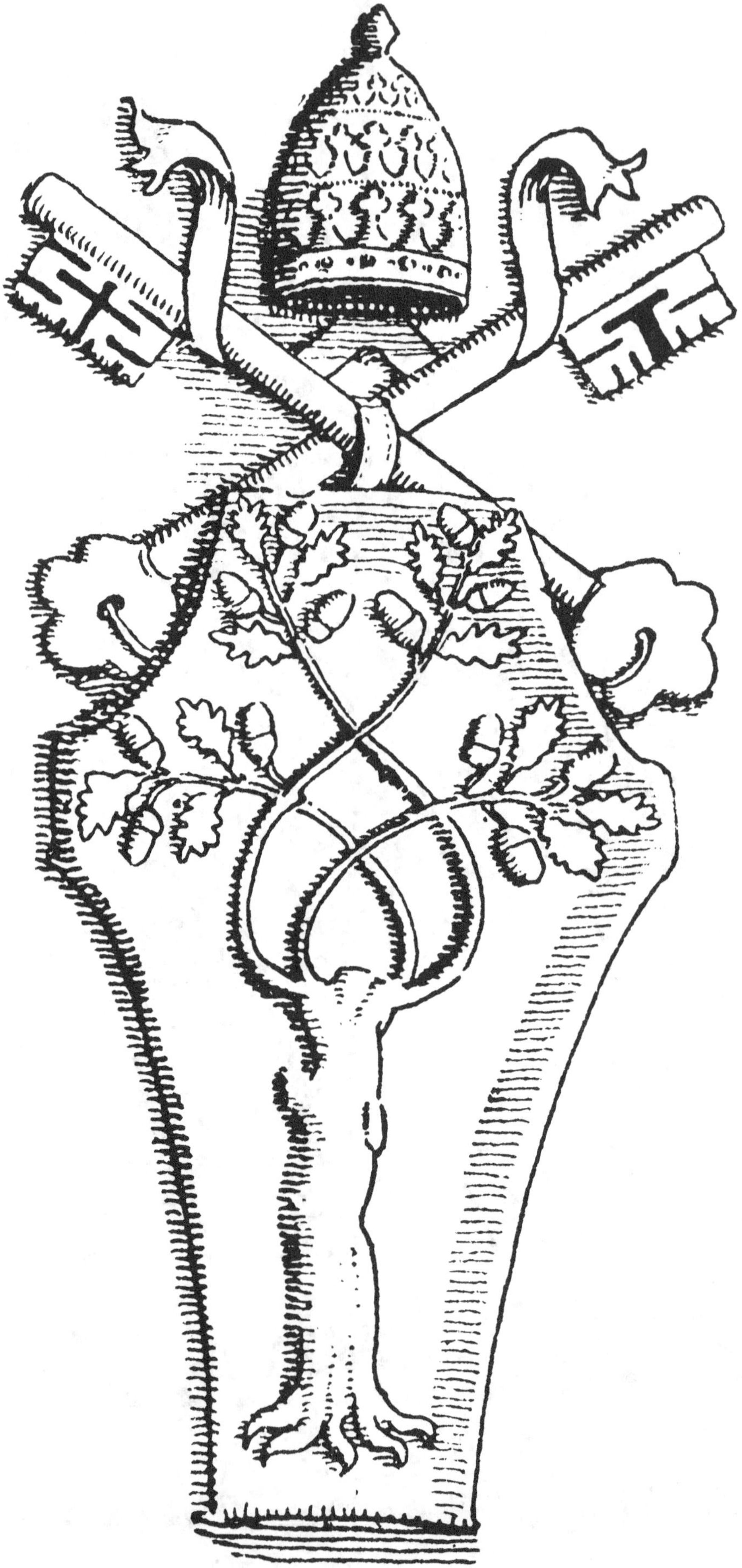

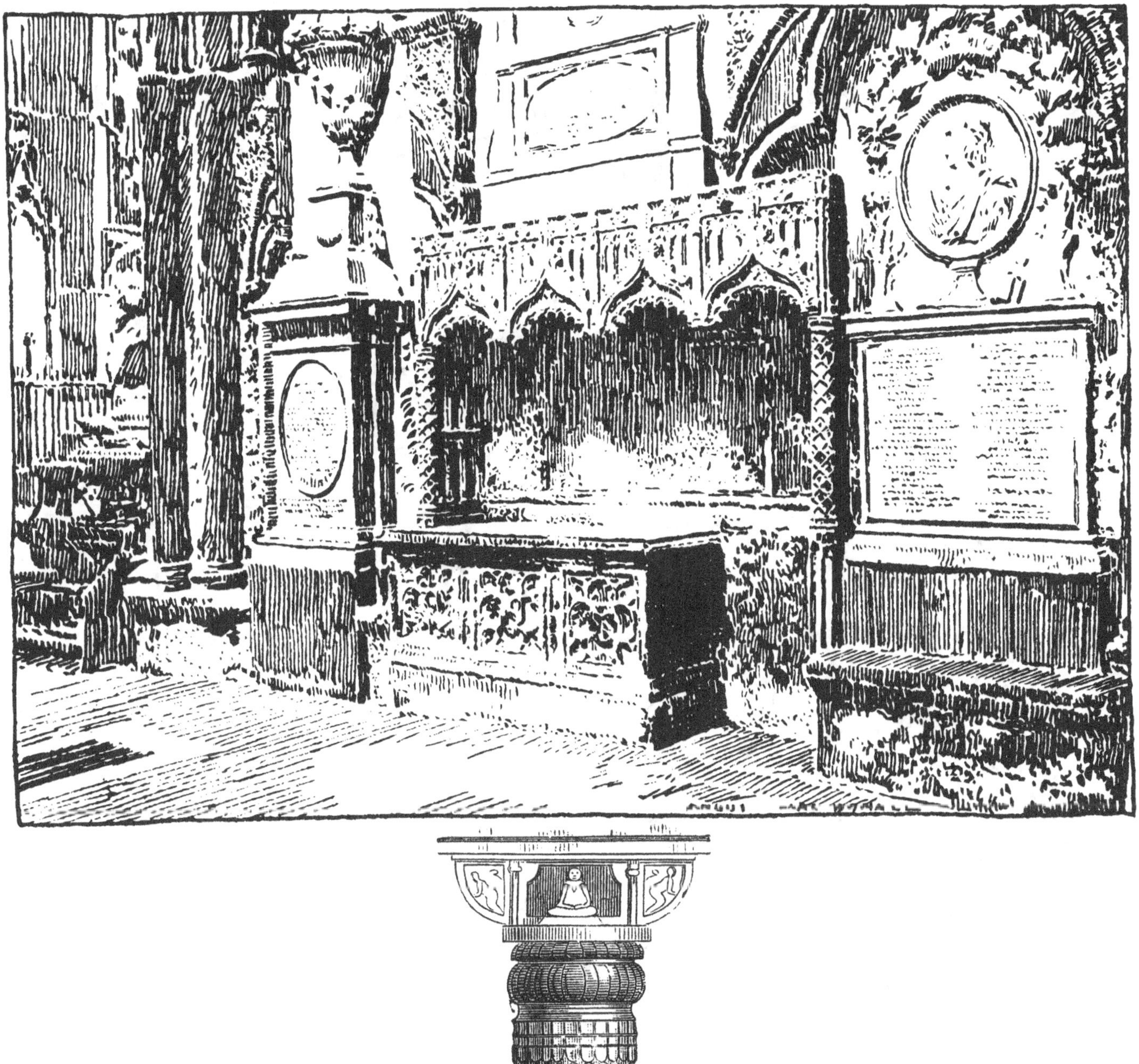

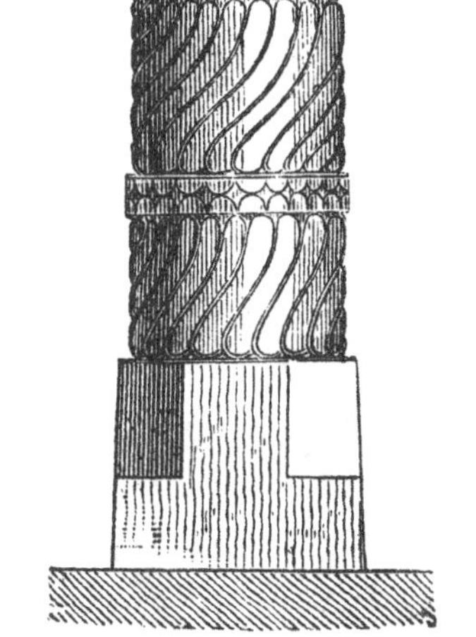

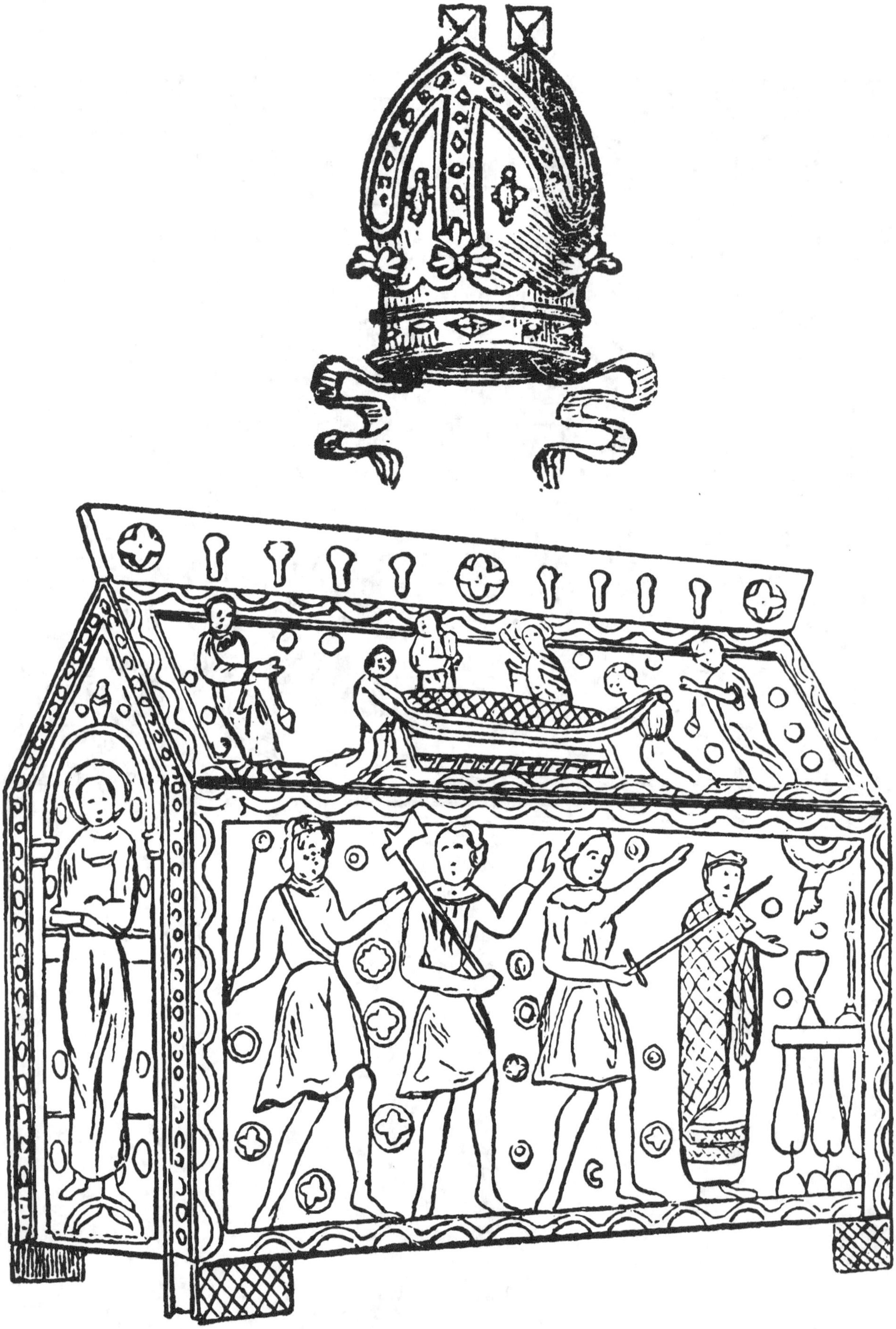

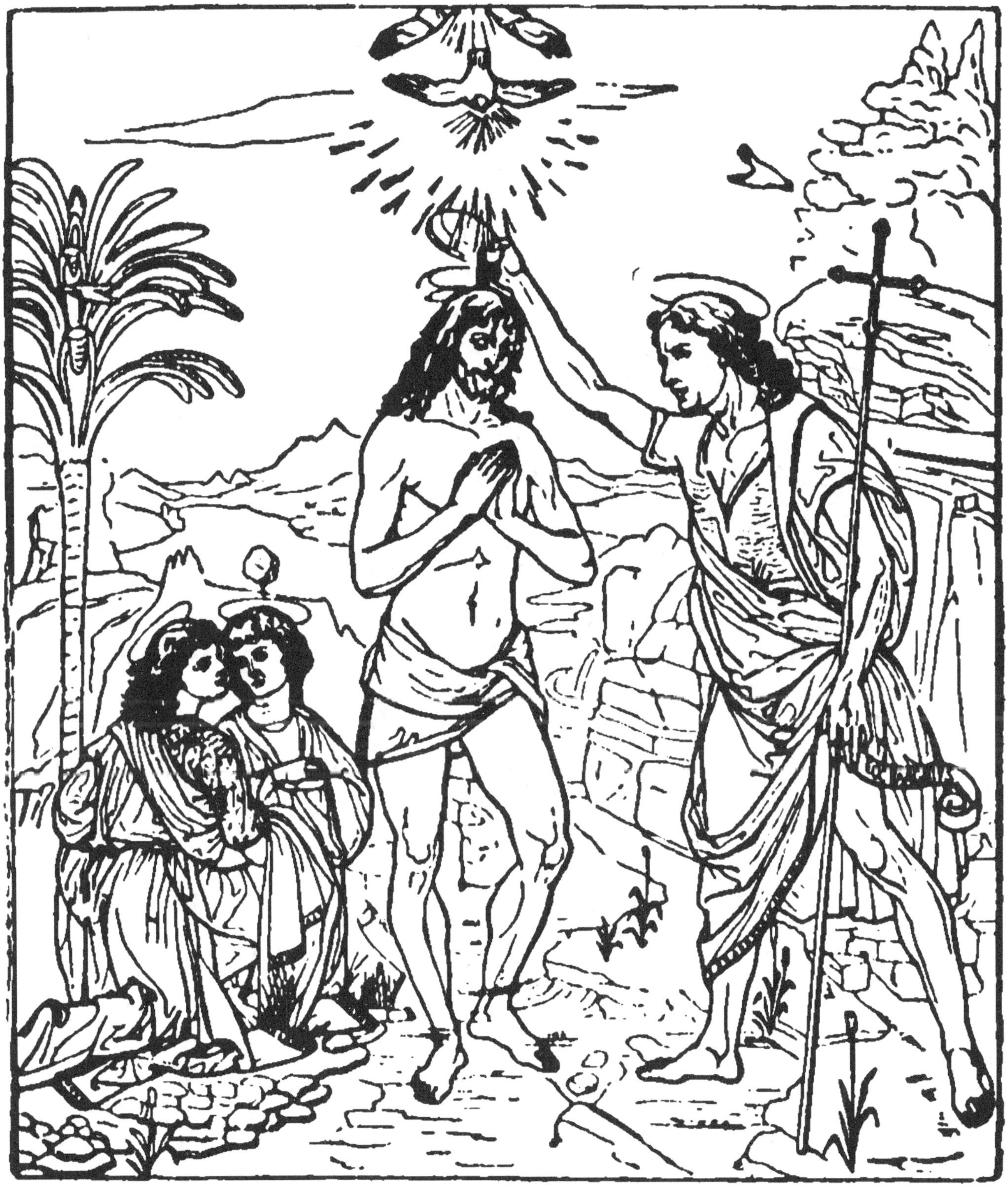

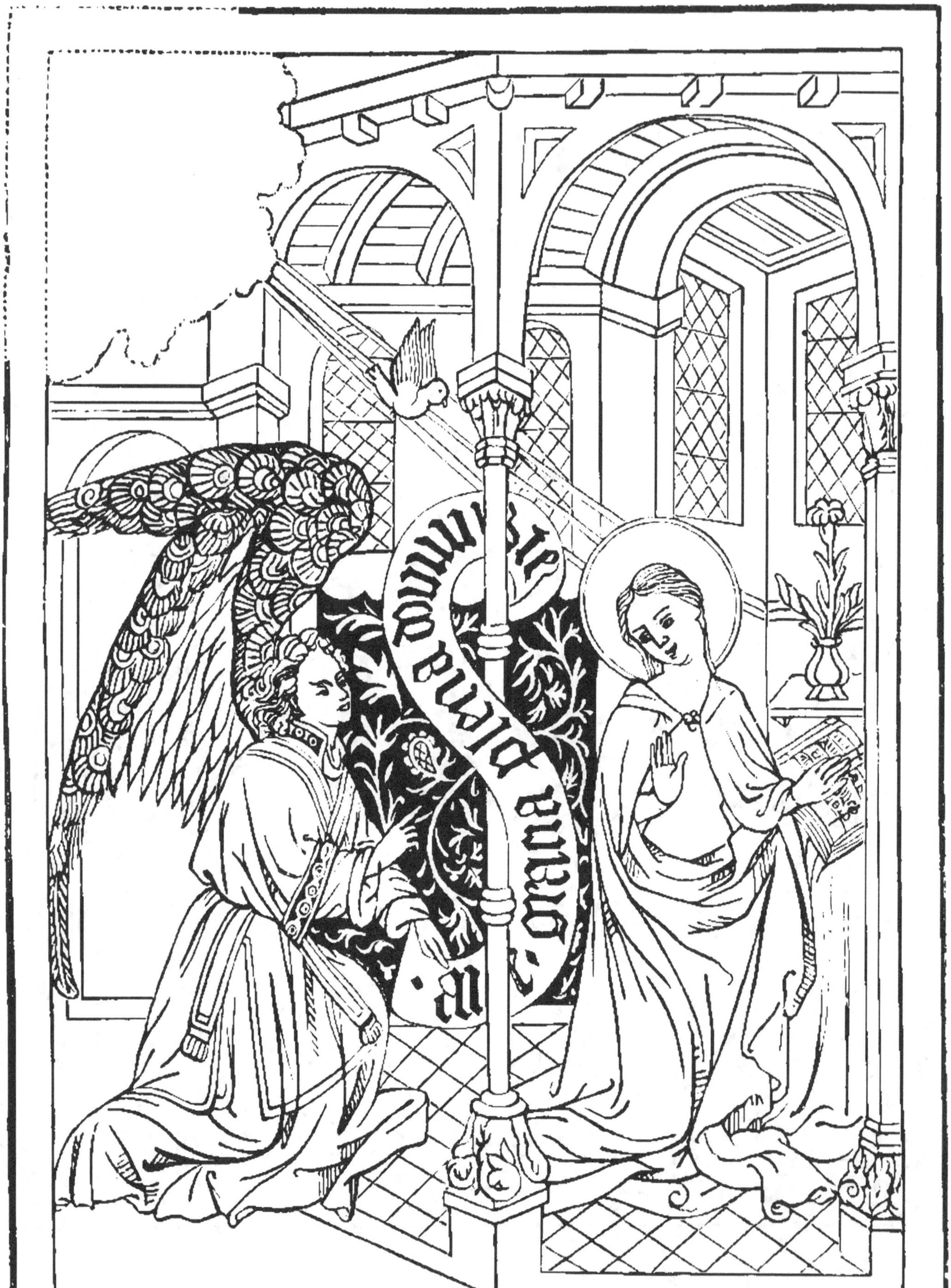

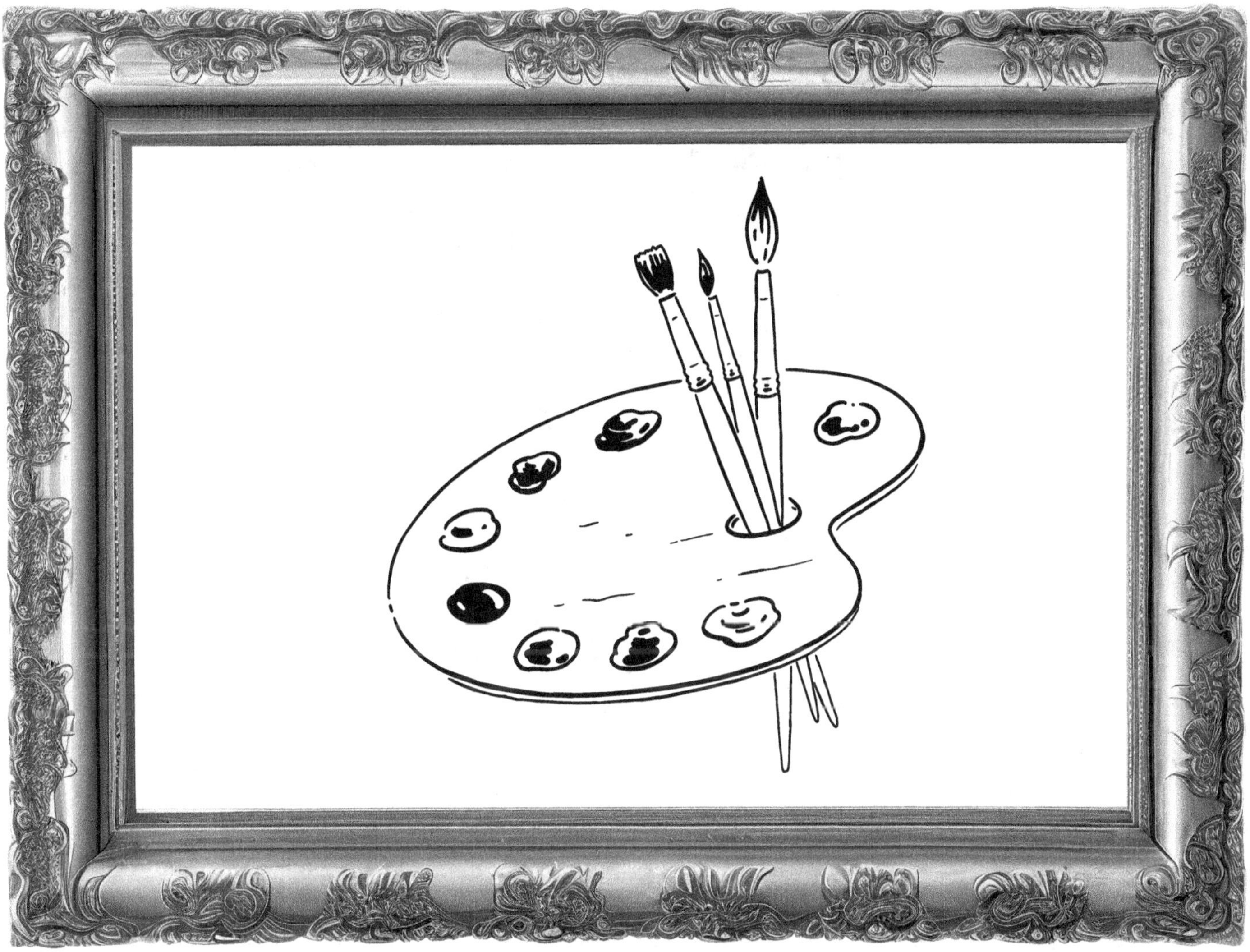

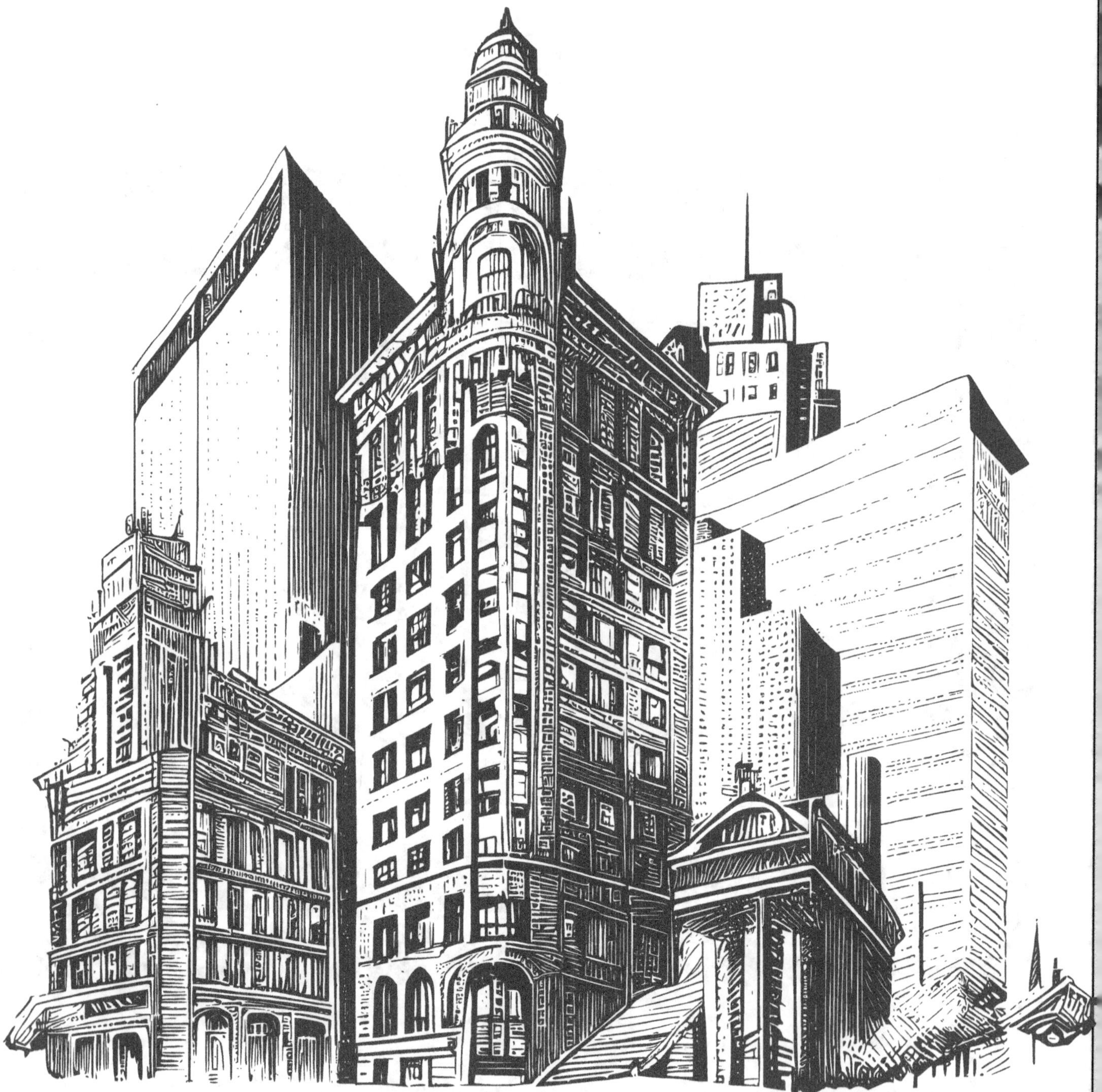

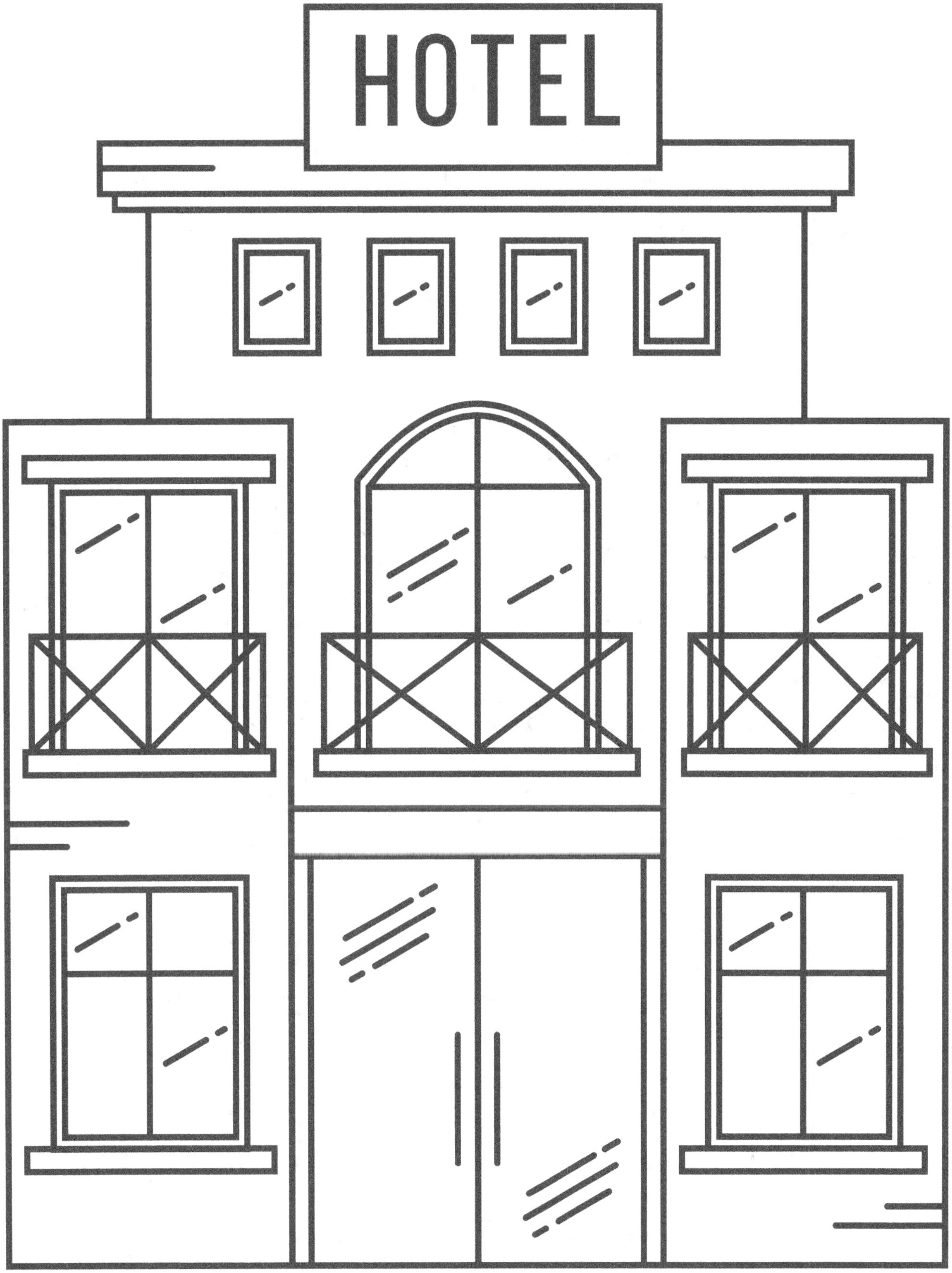
HOTEL

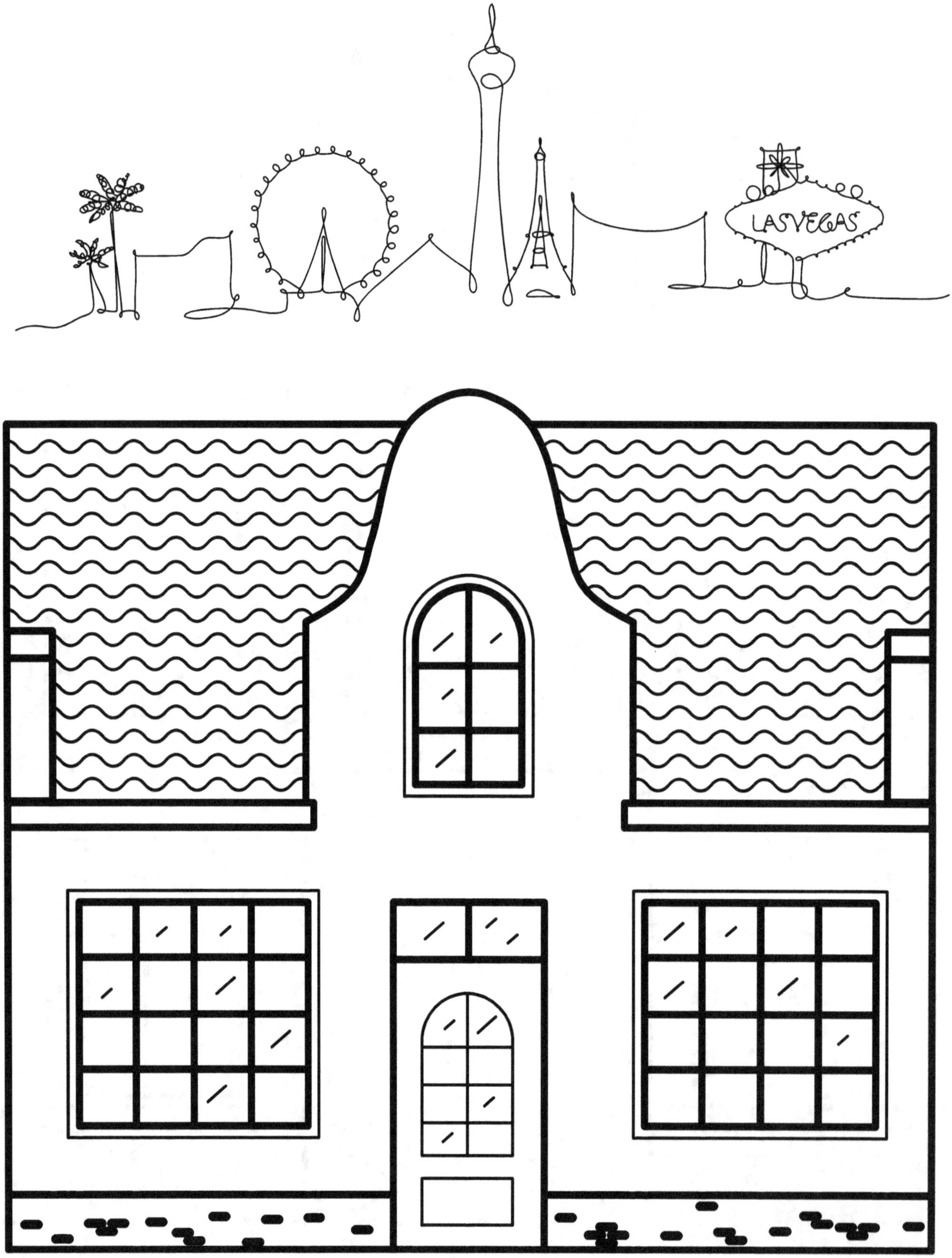
LAS VEGAS

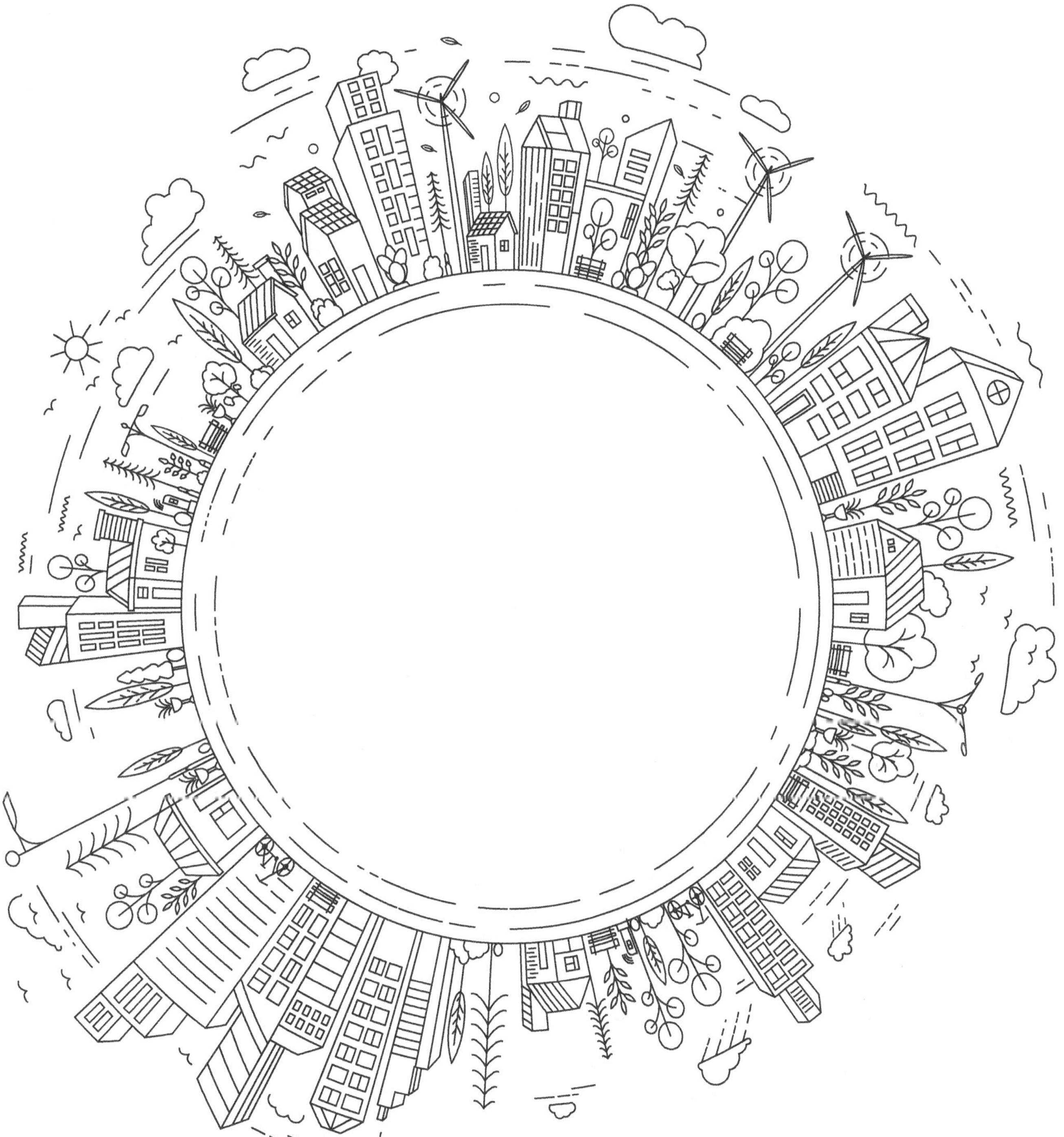

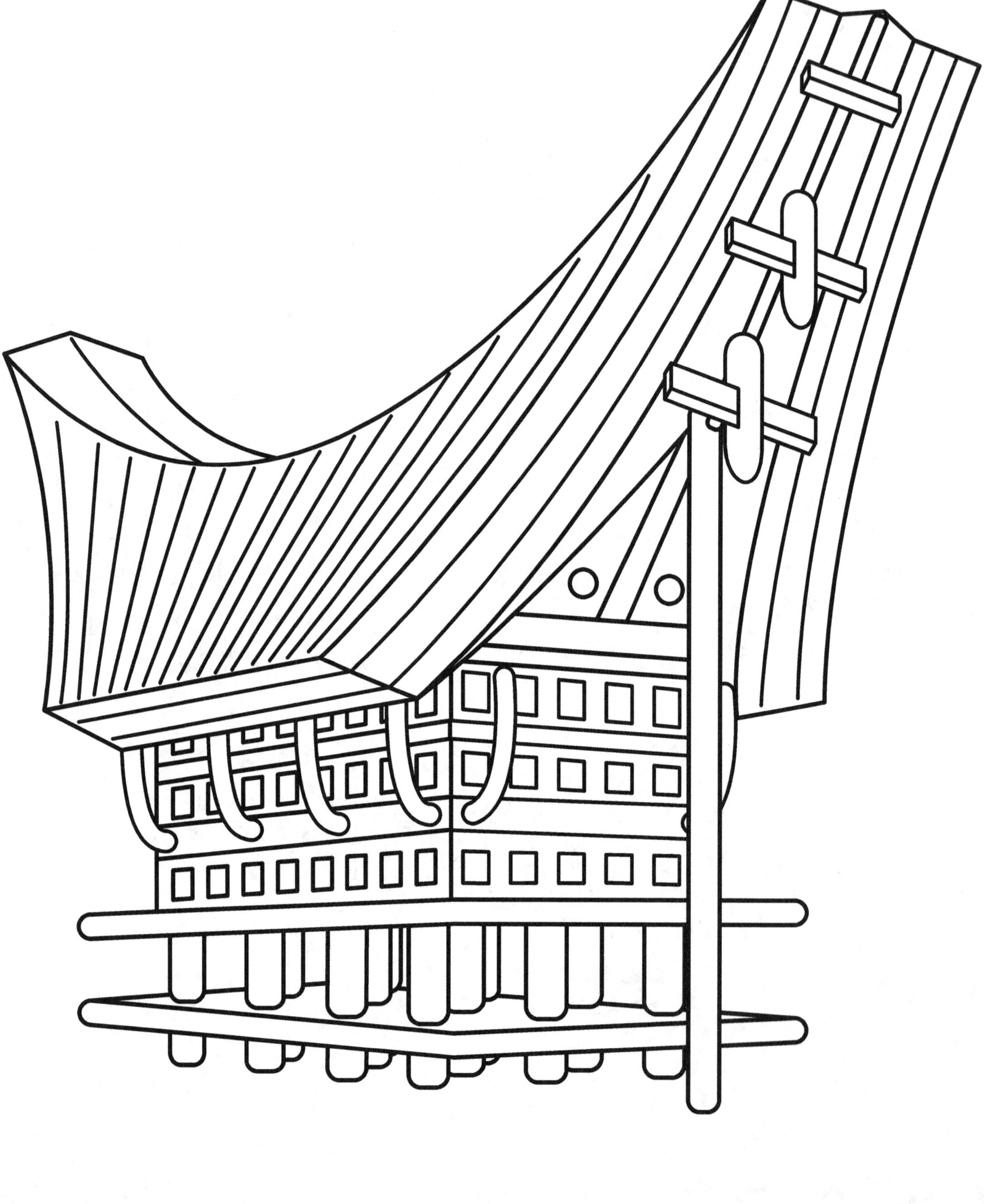

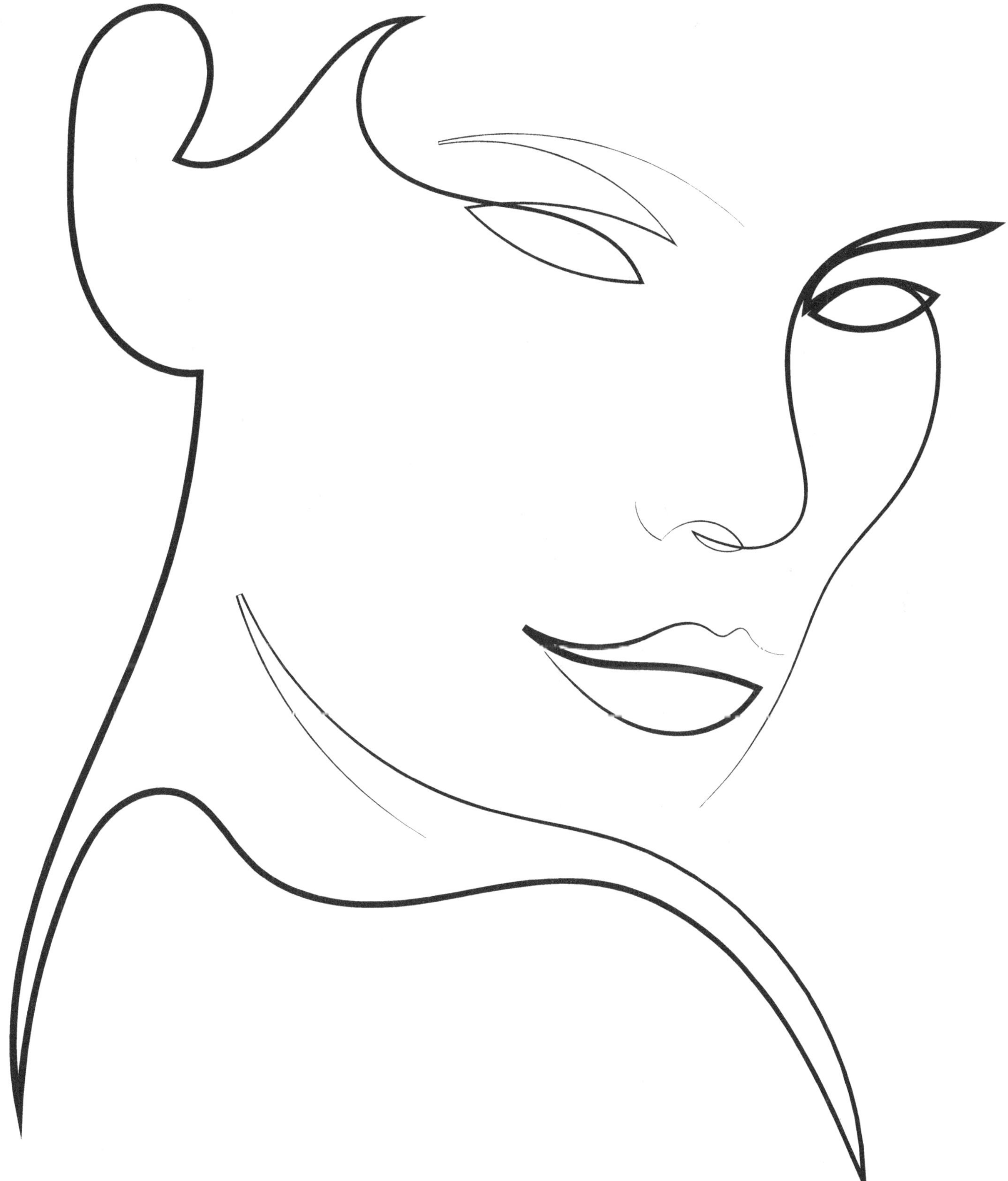

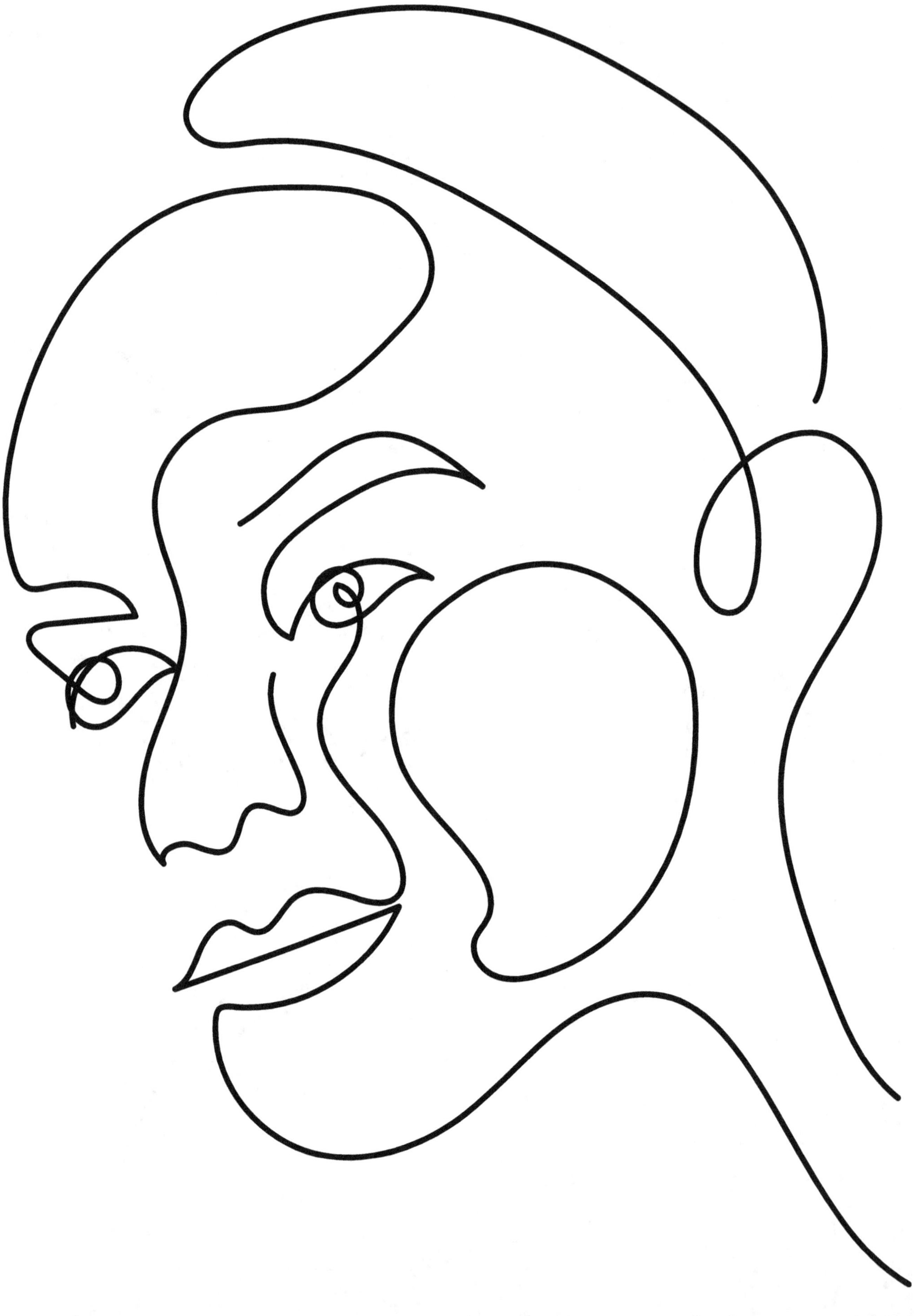

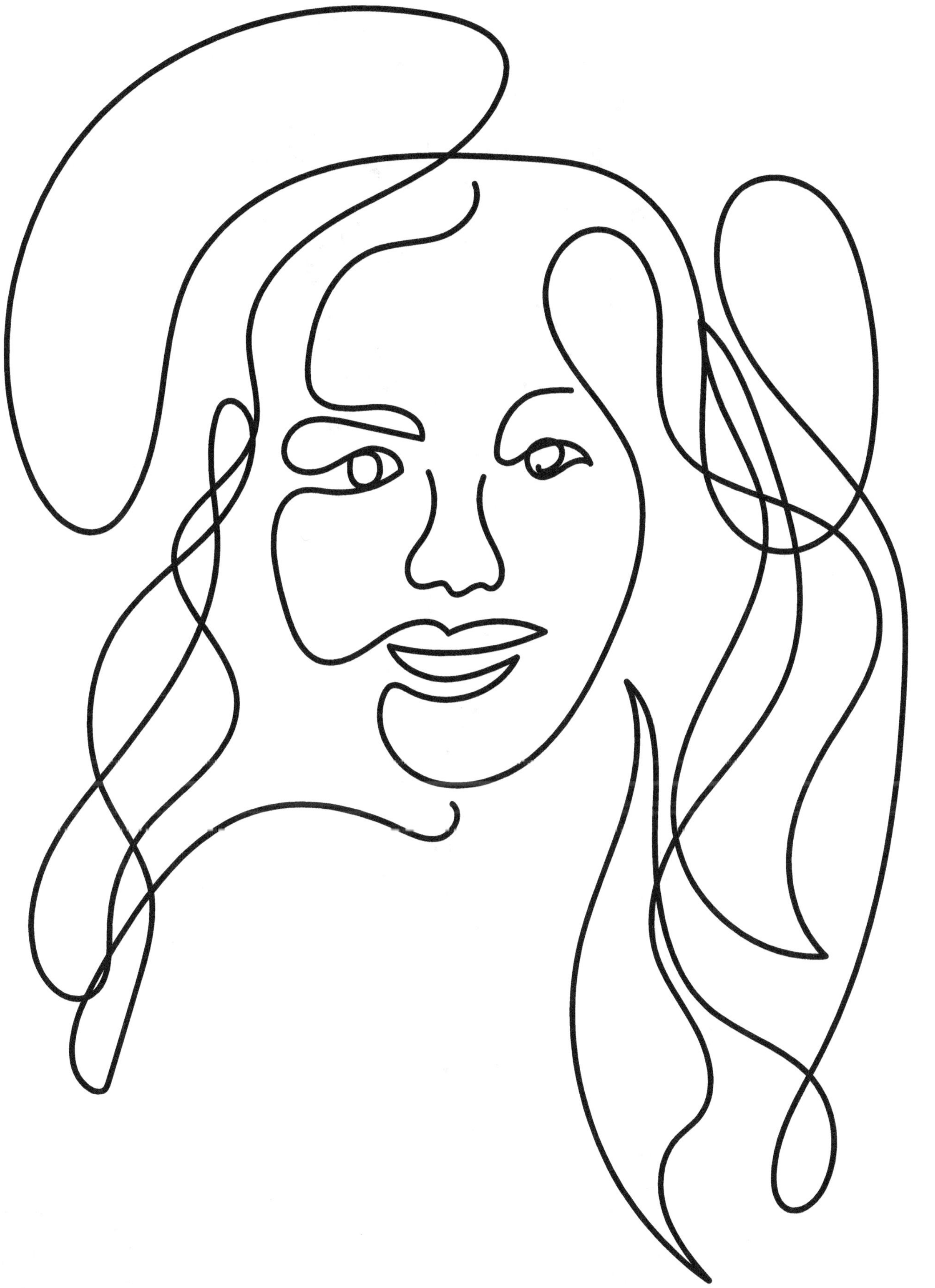

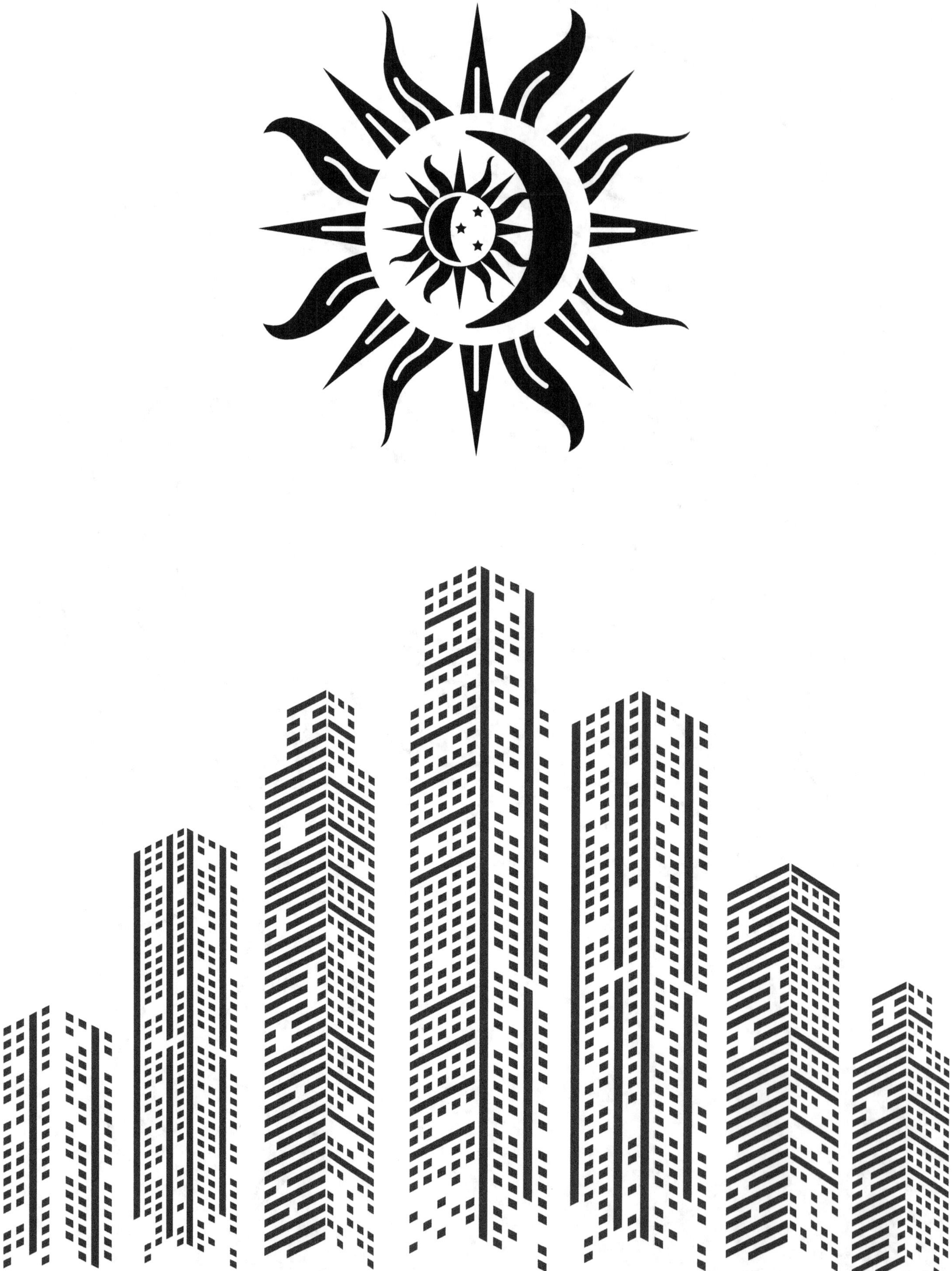

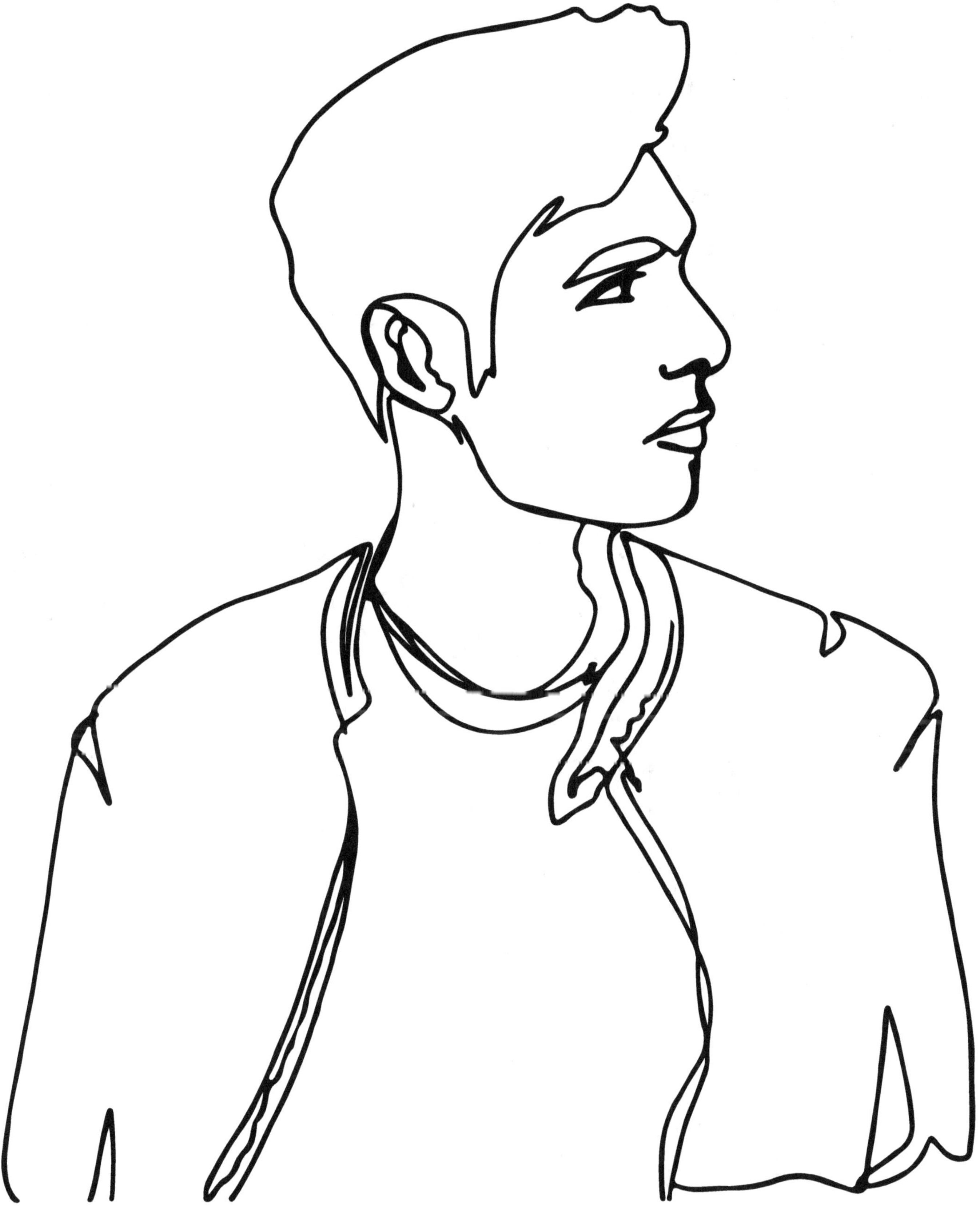

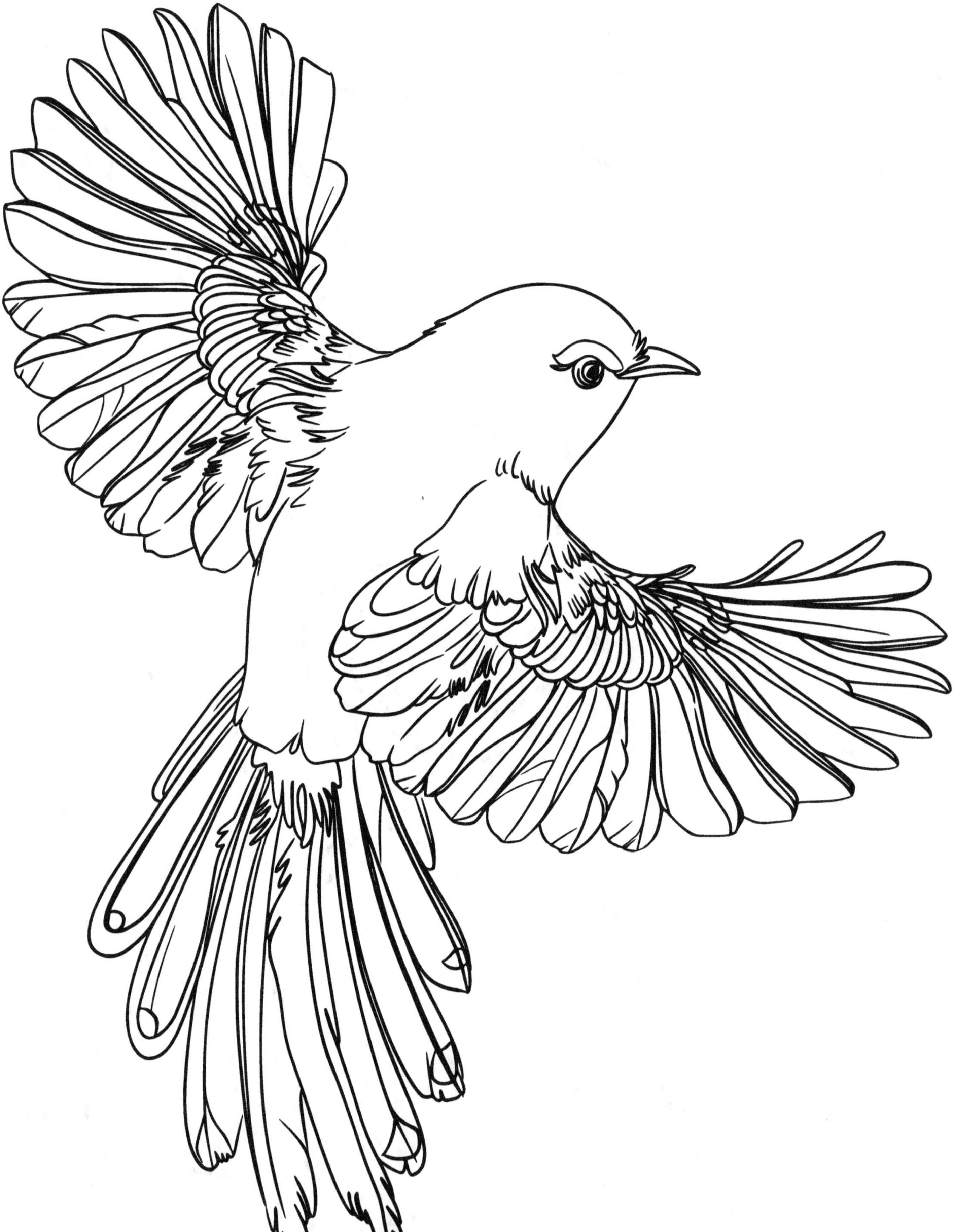

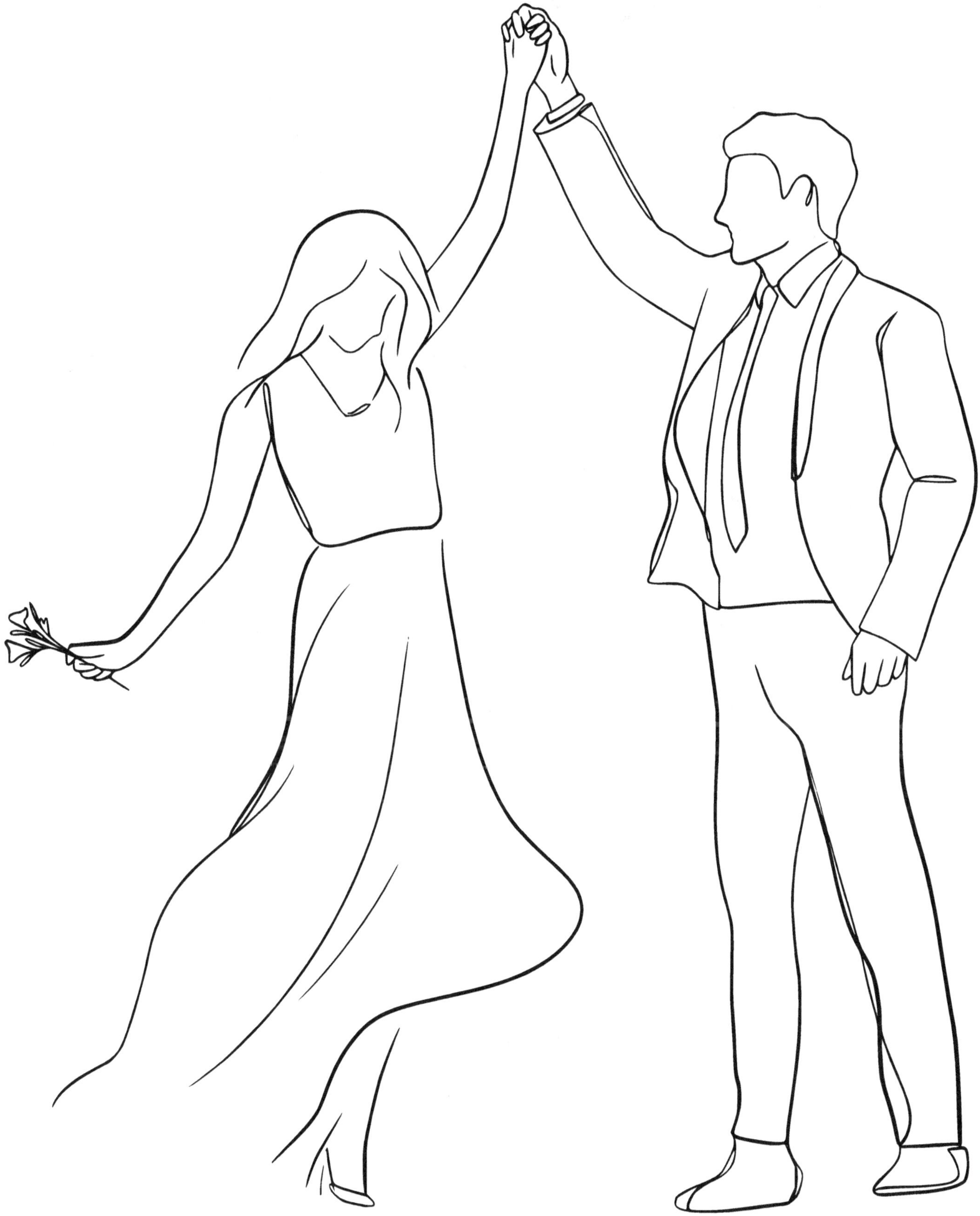

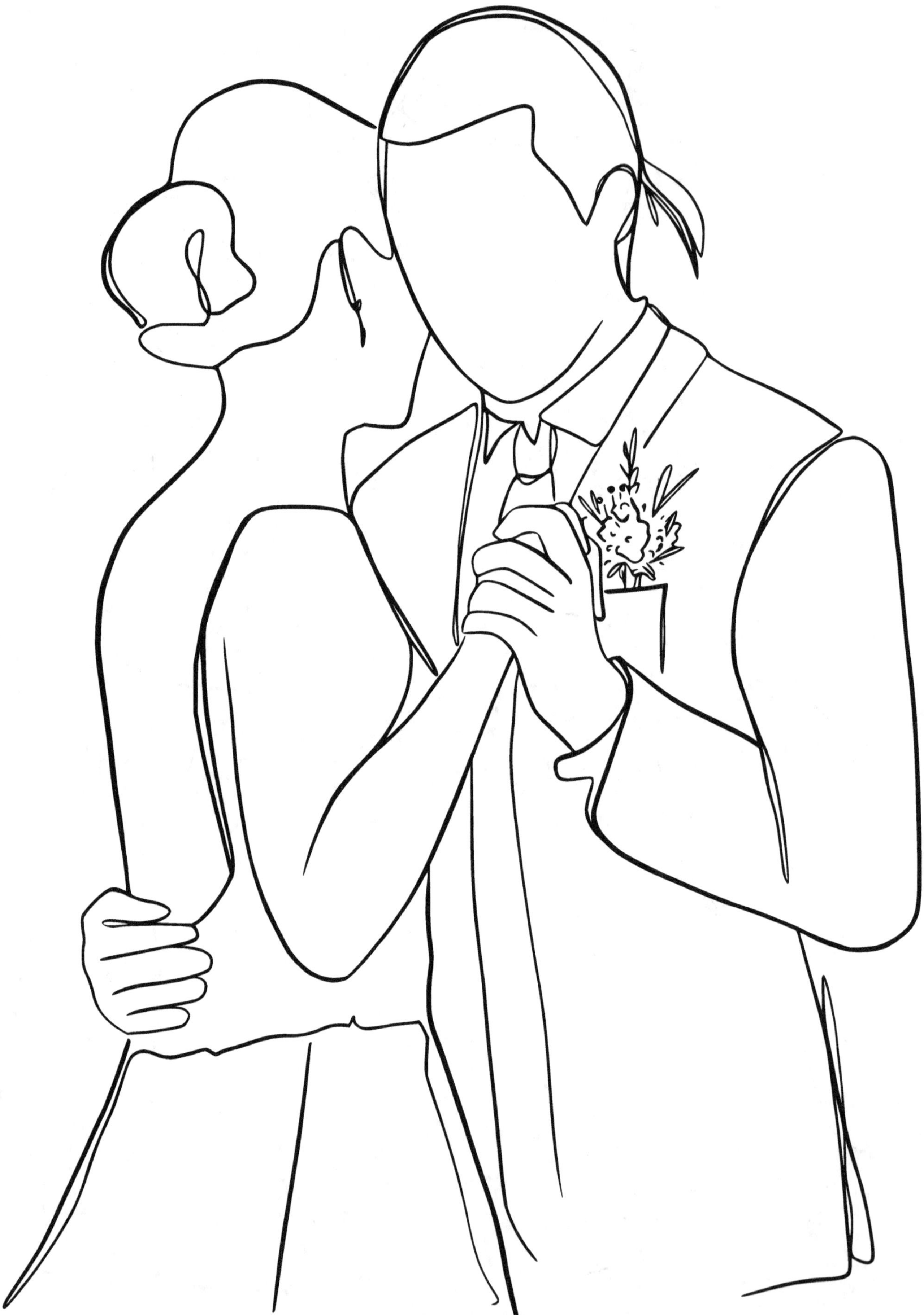

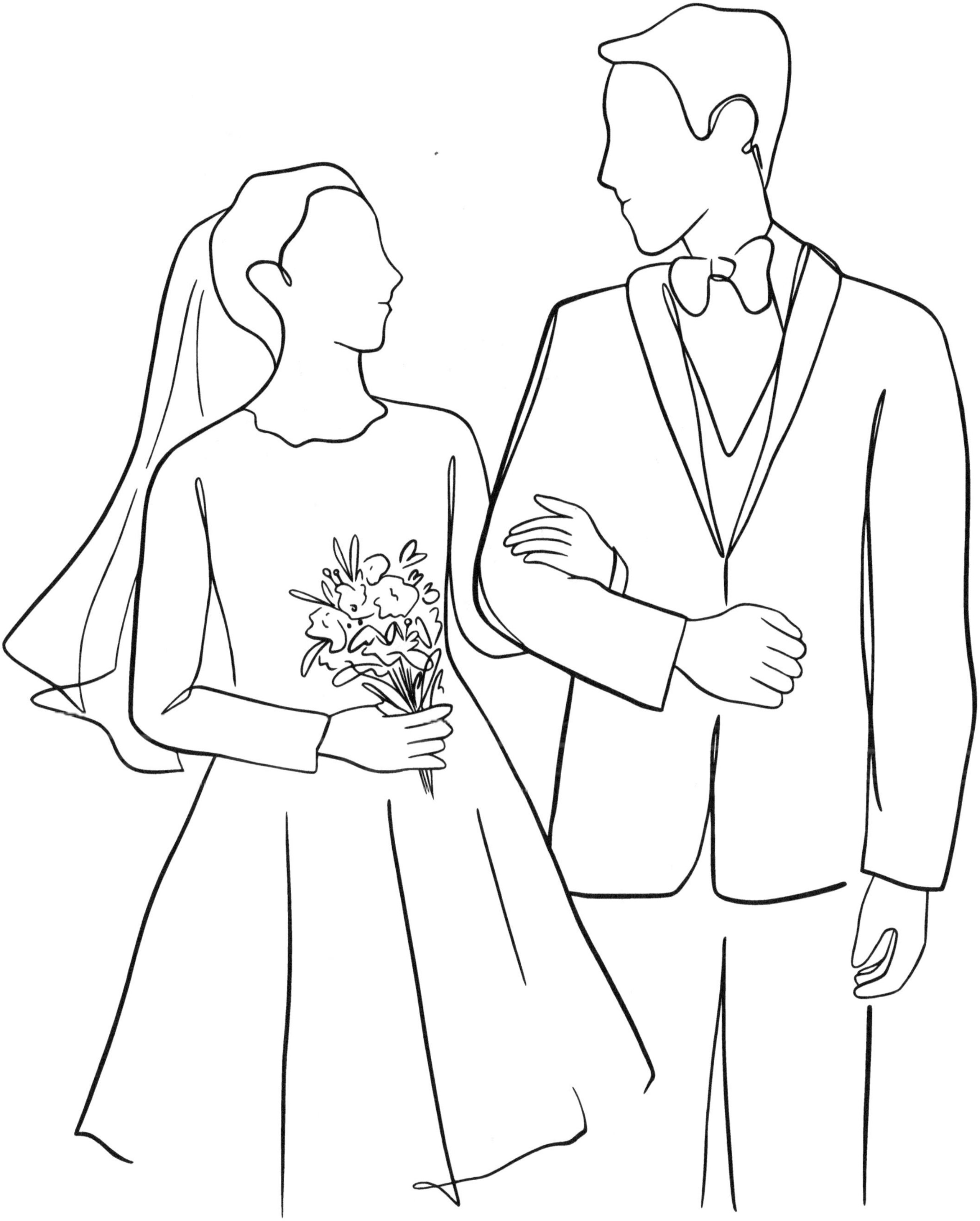

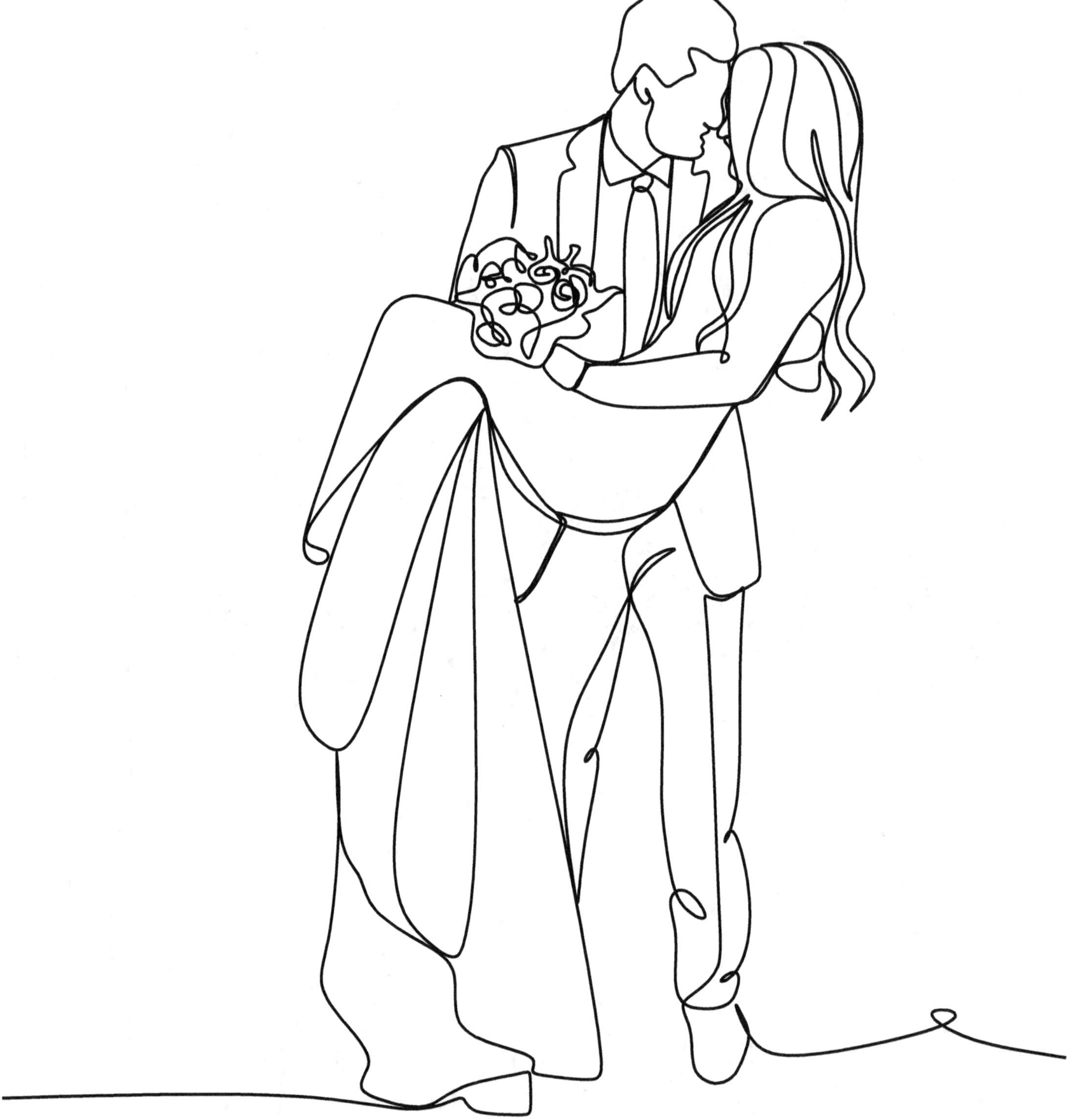

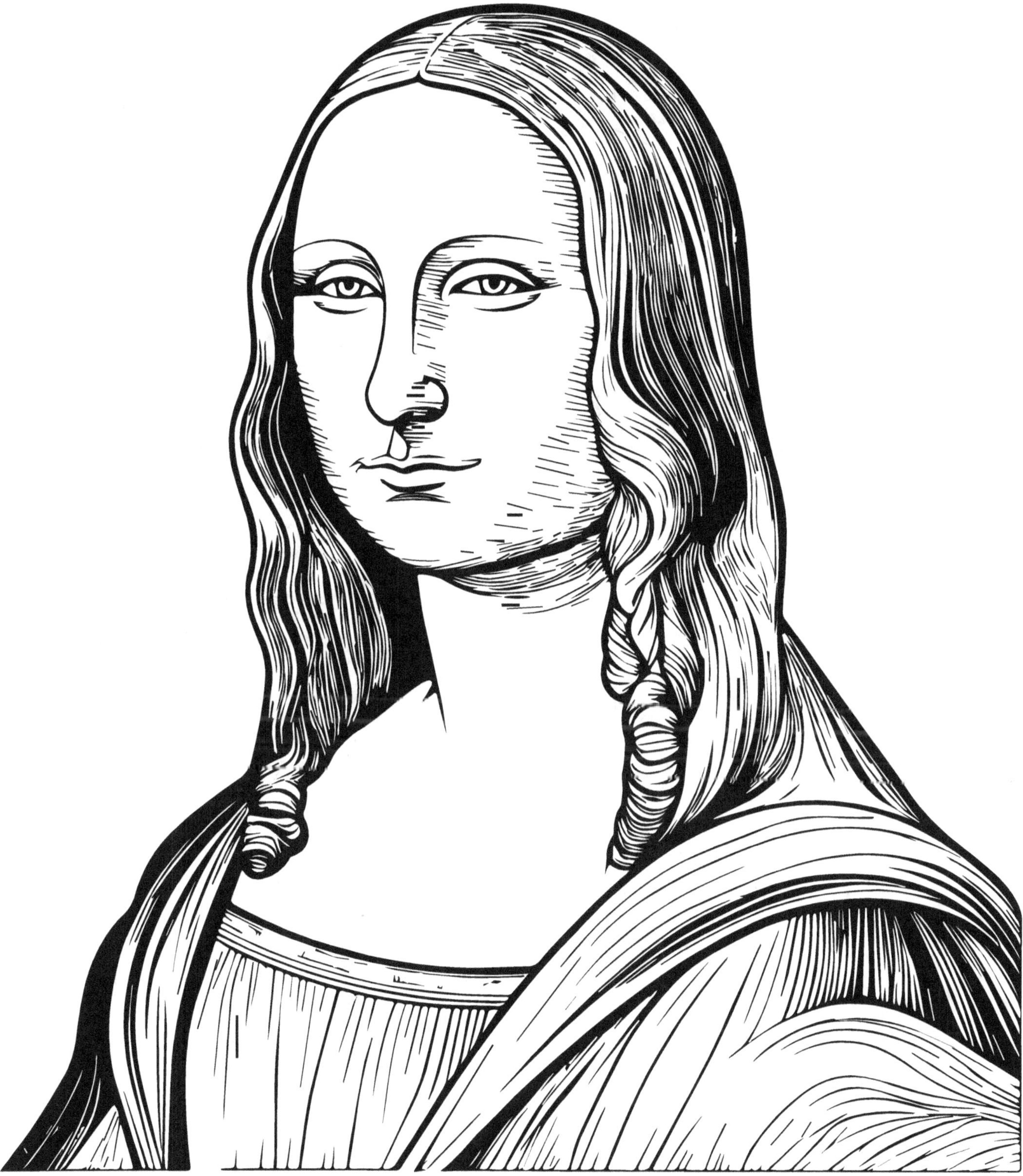

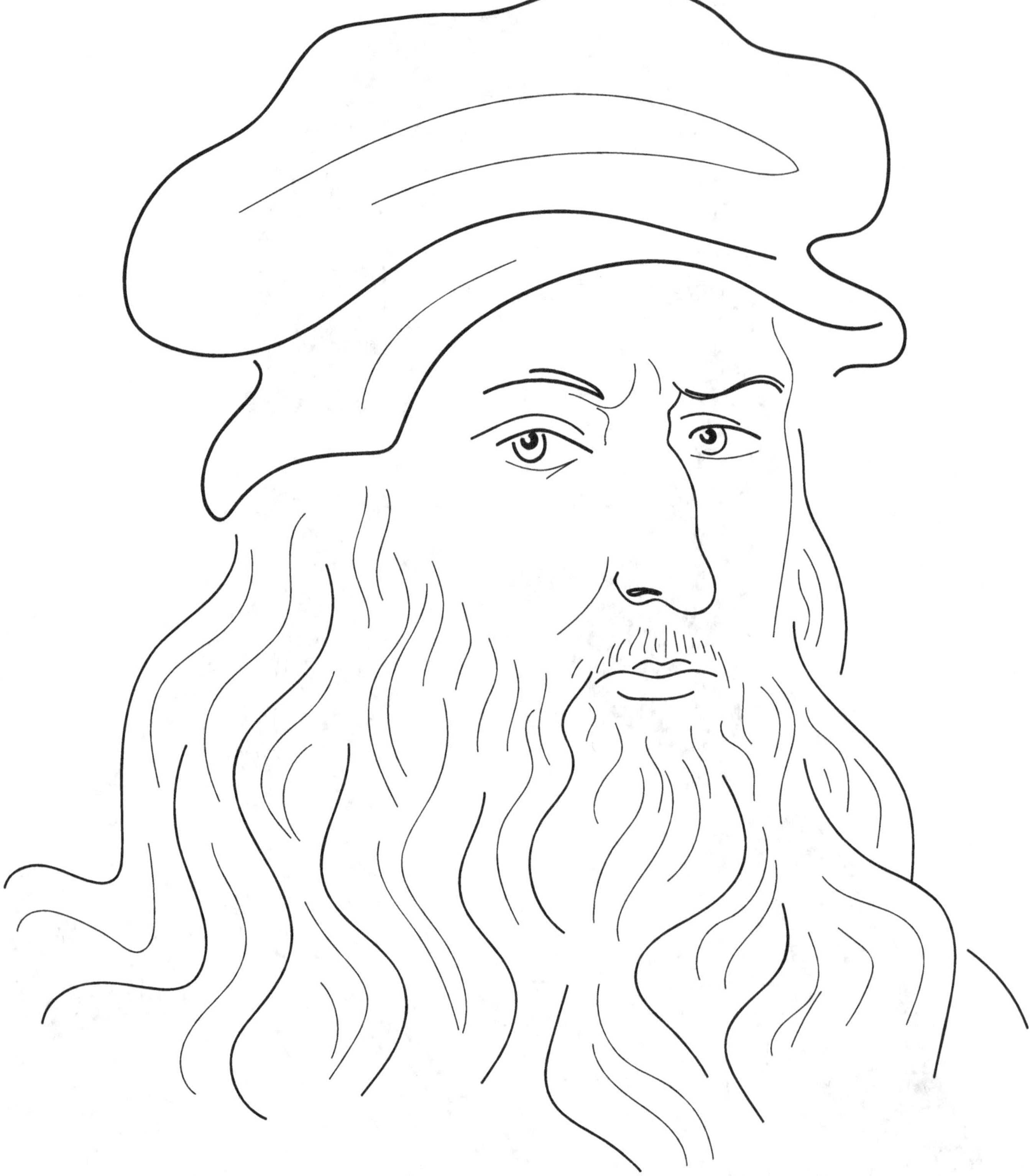

www.ingramcontent.com/pod-product-compliance
Lightning Source LLC
Chambersburg PA
CBHW082224290526
45794CB00009B/3664